A WORLD OF QUILTS

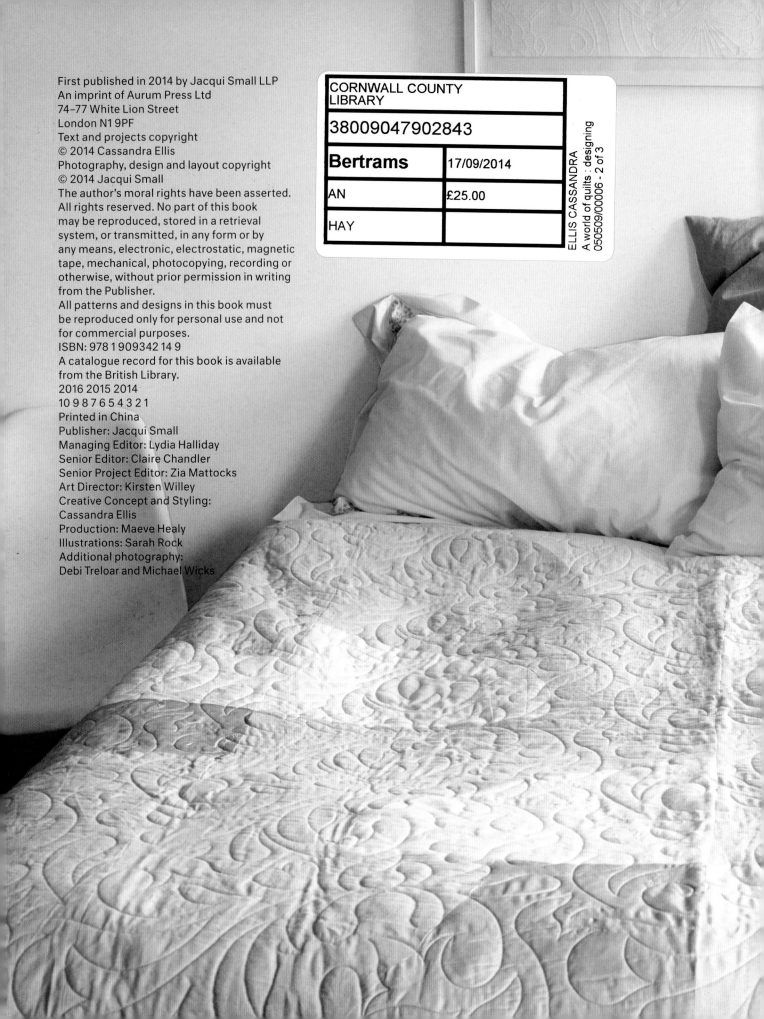

First published in 2014 by Jacqui Small LLP
An imprint of Aurum Press Ltd
74–77 White Lion Street
London N1 9PF
Text and projects copyright
© 2014 Cassandra Ellis
Photography, design and layout copyright
© 2014 Jacqui Small

ISBN: 978 1 909342 14 9
A catalogue record for this book is available
from the British Library.
2016 2015 2014
10 9 8 7 6 5 4 3 2 1
Printed in China
Publisher: Jacqui Small
Managing Editor: Lydia Halliday
Senior Editor: Claire Chandler
Senior Project Editor: Zia Mattocks
Art Director: Kirsten Willey
Creative Concept and Styling:
Cassandra Ellis
Production: Maeve Healy
Illustrations: Sarah Rock
Additional photography:
Debi Treloar and Michael Wicks

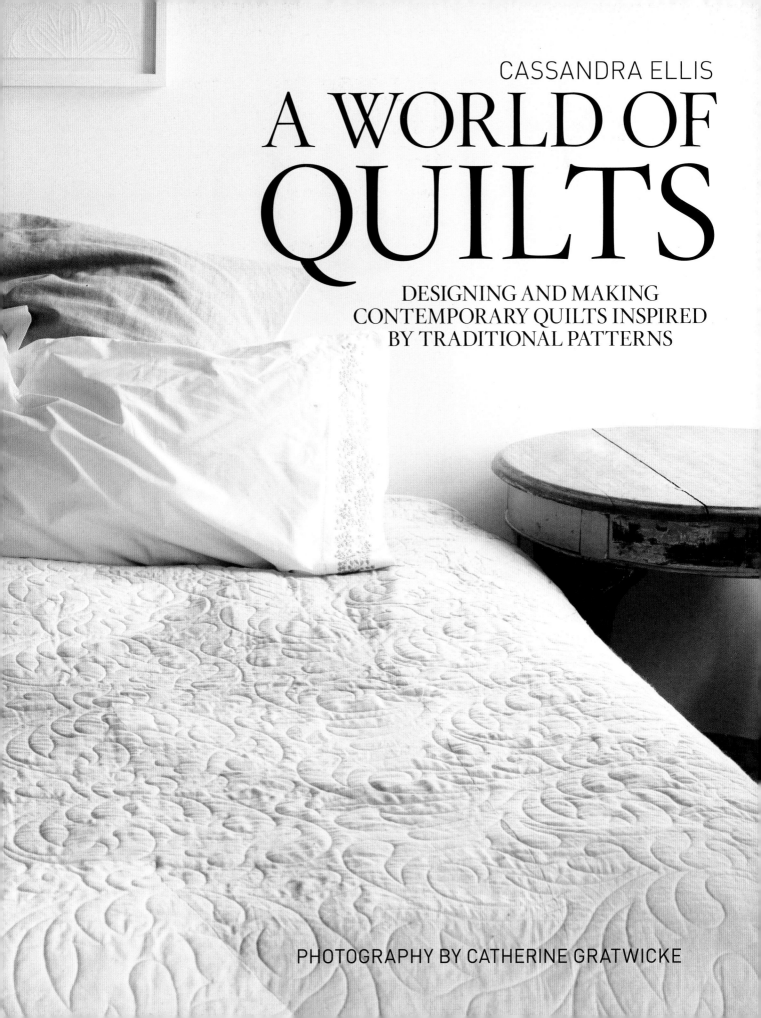

CASSANDRA ELLIS

A WORLD OF QUILTS

DESIGNING AND MAKING
CONTEMPORARY QUILTS INSPIRED
BY TRADITIONAL PATTERNS

PHOTOGRAPHY BY CATHERINE GRATWICKE

CONTENTS

INTRODUCTION

I AM A SELF-TAUGHT QUILTER. I have always known how to sew and make (and improvise). I understand what fabric is and the inherent qualities of each type, and I am good at maths. I have always been fairly obsessed about the idea of 'home' and how people live. I used to own a homewares store where we designed and made all of our goods, and it was while searching for a quilt I would want to make and sell that everything collided. I realized that quilts were – and still could be – the absolute summation of homes, families, communities and individuals. They were practical and very, very personal, which meant they became completely precious to the individual and family. Quilts represented both the maker's creativity and their family's history. As well as a means to provide warmth, quilts could be the ultimate storytellers.

My passion for quilts was fuelled as I began working out how they were constructed. I needed to understand the practical element so that, once that knowledge was safely absorbed, I could happily move on to the anthropological elements that add the magic ingredient. I looked at many books and visited galleries and historic houses to find and understand the quilts that I loved. I was as emotionally moved by the quilts of Gee's Bend in Alabama as by the simple beauty of Welsh Wholecloth quilts. I rummaged through many Indian Kantha quilts and got terribly excited by the Pojagi quilts from Korea. These quilts were obviously technically brilliant but also spirited and uplifting. The quilt books I read were not technical books, but books based on the history of quilts and their makers – covering both anthropology and design. I also devoured books on fashion design and construction, as well as books on sociology and art, because they all seemed relevant to the quilts I wanted to make.

This desire to understand the maker still excites me when designing and making quilts or teaching others. I love that I can see the hand of the maker and understand history, culture and political movements through the women (and men) who made the quilts. I am more interested in someone's choice of colour palette than his or her stitching prowess. I have seen quilts of aching beauty made from little more than scraps, and many more 'wonky' quilts that are truly moving.

Most of these makers were also self-taught; they relied on their intuition and personal creativity to produce quilts that performed the essential duty of keeping

their families warm. The quilts they made were also works of great beauty and represented a time and place where communities were built and friendships were formed. These groups shared techniques and styles with each other, and, as they moved around the world, their quilt designs continued to adjust and change.

Many quilts were created by women who lived through extreme hardship, sometimes poverty and isolation of every kind. New beginnings and old limitations have resulted in quilts of breathtaking beauty. Their quilts defined them as a tribe within a period in history and gave them a voice when they had no voice of their own. Function may have been the key motivator, but they allowed the women to communicate their individual creativity and values. Some of these quilts have now been elevated to pieces of art, but their reason for existence was always about need. Their families needed shelter and comfort, and this is what I find most compelling and poignant about quilts. Find a story and a quilt that move you. Do not fret over your stitching skills or be anxious about your choice of fabric. Most of all, don't give a moment's thought to whether you feel you are creative. Just make.

I like to think this book is an encouraging and uplifting entry into the world of quilting. There are 25 different designs based on the quilts I love, from around the globe. Between them they will teach you many skills, but also help you to create the quilt you would like to make. Adapt them to suit your own requirements and aesthetic desire. Revel in your style of making, but be buoyed by the knowledge you have gained. It is a good idea to read the Quilt Masterclass (see page 164) first, as I think it may demystify what a quilt is and help you plan what you want to make and how to go about it. All you need are the tools and an understanding of the glorious craftsmanship of quilt-making, and you are ready to create something practical, incredibly personal and extremely precious.

'For me, quilts have always been about people – their lives, their families and their personal environment.'

QUILT STYLES

POSTAGE STAMP

DO YOU REMEMBER the first time you made something with fabric, a needle and thread? Did your mother or grandmother teach you, or was it your teacher or older sister? Oh, the thrill of the first few stitches and, then, the amazing realization that you could actually make something. We, like hundreds of thousands of girls before us, have learnt to piece squares together using a needle and thread. We discovered that our hands could make and that we could be creative. Perhaps it came to nothing, or perhaps that first foray turned into your first quilt.

Throughout history, Postage Stamp quilts were created as a way of using up the tiniest scraps of fabric left over from other projects or worn-out clothes. The very first quilts weren't always made from squares – any size or shape of patch would do because using every scrap of cloth was important. Squares, however, are the simplest shape to sew with, which made them a perfect tool for teaching girls essential sewing skills. There are many definitions of a true Postage Stamp quilt. Some people are sticklers for 2.5cm squares; others say any small size is fine. I tend to err on the side of the second option, as I think the making is more important than the precision of size.

The repetitive nature of the design meant that these quilts could be sewn with little concentration – important when the mind needed to be quelled or tasked to think of other things. During periods of war, women would often work on these quilts to help pass the time and distract their thoughts – hence, they are often known as 'worry' quilts.

The Postage Stamp quilt is also extremely portable, as small sections could be carried and worked on in any free moment. They were often pieced with no set pattern in mind, if they were to be used as simple utilitarian quilts. However, Postage Stamp quilts also became a source of great competition, as makers sought to demonstrate their stitching prowess, and many designs and patterns have been created over the years.

I made a Postage Stamp blanket as a child, and I guess the simplicity of it captured my heart. They were happy days of making my small scrappy blanket, and then wrapping either my doll or my dog with it. If I close my eyes, I can take myself there in a second – and that is a lovely memory to hold on to.

QUILT SIZE

60 x 70cm when trimmed and bound. All seam allowances are 1cm and are already built into the cutting sizes.

QUILT TOP

You will need approximately 1m of fabric. This is the perfect quilt project to use scraps – either leftovers from other projects or tiny snippets of extra-special fabric, or both. I used a mixture of silk fragments that I already had – everything from the delicate lining of an old French jacket to silk sari borders. I also hand-dyed silk habotai with rosehips to use as a subtle plain.

QUILT BACKING

You will need approximately 90cm of fabric. The finished size should be at least 80 x 90cm, so you can use anything you have to hand for this project.

BINDING

You will need approximately 0.25m of fabric. You can use fabric scraps from the quilt top – I used the woven edging from one of the saris.

OTHER MATERIALS

WADDING of your choice, 80 x 90cm.
SEWING THREAD 100 per cent cotton all-purpose thread is best, in a neutral colour.
QUILTING THREAD 100 per cent cotton quilting thread in a colour of your choice.

CUT YOUR FABRIC

This is a very simple quilt to cut indeed.

Cut 84 squares measuring 7 x 7cm in a light-toned fabric or mix of fabrics.

Cut 84 squares measuring 7 x 7cm in a dark-toned fabric or mix of fabrics.

You can use four different fabrics to create a simple chequerboard effect, or mix a number of fabrics together, just balancing light and dark compositions. I used four fabrics as the base, but added in a handful of other fabrics to place in a 'random' fashion through the quilt.

Put your squares in two piles – one light and one dark – and you are ready to sew.

SEW YOUR QUILT TOP

Select your first four squares – two from the light pile and two from the dark pile. Join them in alternate pairs. Now join the two pairs together, matching the centre seams and alternating the tones. Press the seams. Your first block is complete.

Make another 41 blocks of four squares each.

Lay the blocks down, six rows across and seven rows down. If you have used a variety of fabrics, rearrange the blocks to find a layout you like.

Sew the first six blocks together in a horizontal row, taking care to match the centre seams. Press the seams and trim the threads. Repeat for the remaining six rows.

Sew the seven rows together, matching the centre seams. Press the seams and trim the threads. Your quilt top is complete.

SEW YOUR QUILT BACKING

Cut a piece of fabric 80 x 90cm, or piece together fabric scraps to this size.

BUILD YOUR QUILT

Put your quilt sandwich together in your preferred way (see page 182). After you have marked any necessary quilting lines, machine- or hand-quilt using your favourite technique (see page 184). Trim the backing and wadding so that the edges are even and your quilt is square. Finally, make and attach the binding (see page 186).

MAKE IT YOURS

This is a quilt you can easily hand-stitch. It is very portable and a good starter project for anyone who hasn't sewn before. Indeed, it is perfect for children, as they can easily create something for their own room, or for their dolls or pets.

You can make this quilt any size you like and use random squares if you prefer that to a light-and-dark combination. The process can be applied to any sized square, but I think it looks precious when they are tiny.

Finished quilt top measures: 62 x 72cm

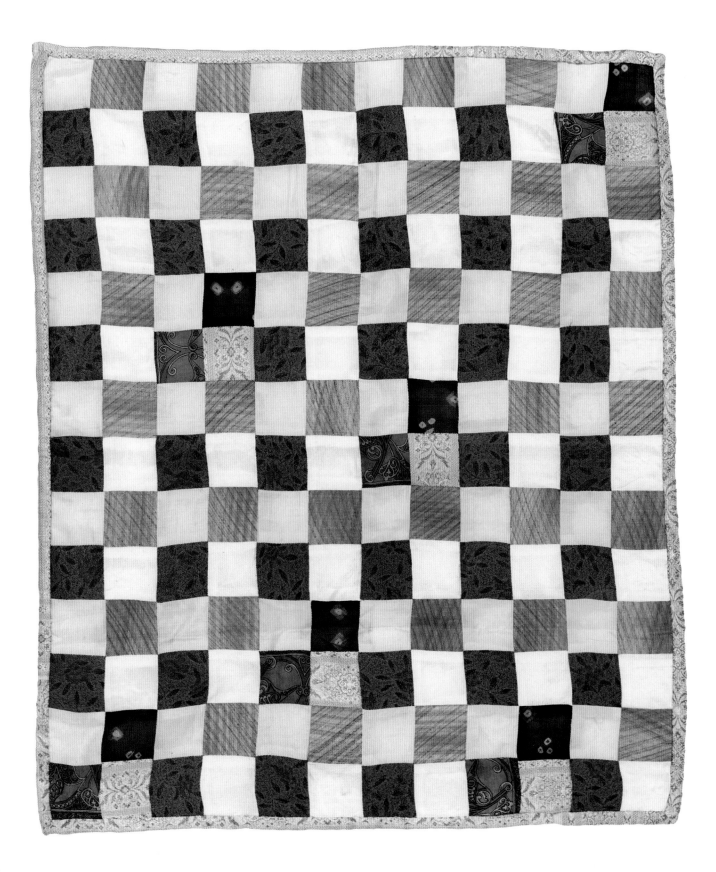

DRUNKARD'S PATH

WITH A NAME like Drunkard's Path, you would assume there is a fascinating back-story to this quilt. Some historians purport delightful tales; others vehemently deny the very same. The names of quilt patterns were often indigenous to a religion, ethnic group, family or even an individual. As these quilts travelled the world, they slowly transformed into new designs with new names to suit the new life and place. Their history was often not recorded or dated with any certainty. For a simple block, Drunkard's Path has a much-disputed historical provenance.

The pattern traditionally comprises only two colours and two simple pieces, although it does involve sewing curves. The initial design was first seen in ancient Roman mosaics, but by the eighteenth century it had emerged in England with the name Rob Peter To Pay Paul or Mill Wheel. When the English settlers arrived in the colonies, new names were coined: Wanderer In The Wilderness, Rocky Road and, finally, Drunkard's Path. Amish quilters called this design Solomon's Puzzle, Old Maid's Dilemma or Endless Trail, to fit their own landscape and ideals.

So why Drunkard's Path? It may be simply that the meandering diagonals resemble a drunkard's weaving walk, or it may be something much more innate. Sewing for a cause has always been an important tradition. In America, women made quilts to raise money and awareness, often to support the abolition of slavery or to promote women's rights. As women were prohibited from voting, some believe the Drunkard's Path quilt was a popular way for women to express their opinion on alcohol and its use and abuse by their menfolk.

Some say the Drunkard's Path block was used during the nineteenth century's Underground Railroad movement, a secret network of routes and safe houses used to help African slaves in America escape to the free states. As the movement could not publicly broadcast information about where, when and how runaway slaves could arrive safely at their destination, quilts containing hidden messages to aid safe travel were displayed on a clothesline or over porch railings. It is said that when the Drunkard's Path block was displayed, the runaways would know to zigzag their path to avoid capture.

It may even have been bad luck to piece a Drunkard's Path quilt, as the person who sleeps under this quilt might 'develop a thirst for drink and wander far from home'. Fable or history – it really doesn't matter, as each quilt will have its own story.

I love the graphic element of Drunkard's Path and especially the combination of curves and rigidity. I decided to enlarge the pattern to create a simple but striking version. It is a favourite quilt, I'll admit, and I wonder what its story will be.

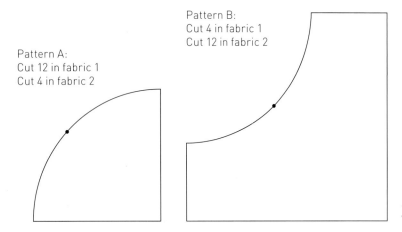

Pattern B:
Cut 4 in fabric 1
Cut 12 in fabric 2

Pattern A:
Cut 12 in fabric 1
Cut 4 in fabric 2

Download the templates for patterns A and B from www.cassandraellis.co.uk/worldofquilts

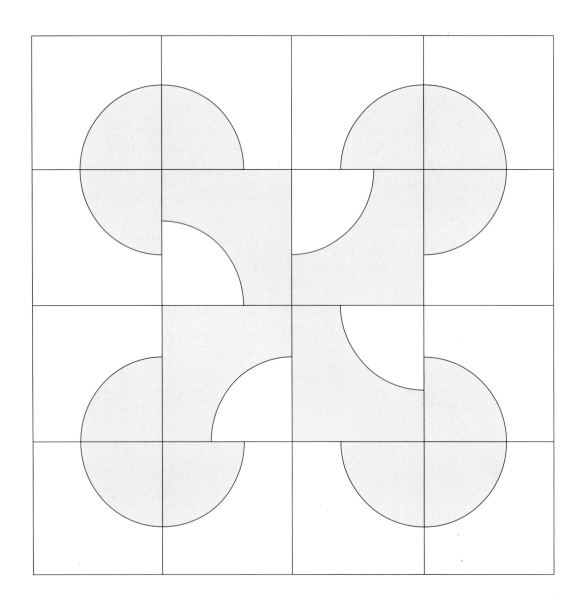

'I love the graphic element of Drunkard's Path and especially the combination of curves and rigidity.'

QUILT SIZE

220 x 220cm when trimmed and bound. All seam allowances are 1cm and are already built into the cutting sizes.

QUILT TOP

The Drunkard's Path design is planned with two fabrics. I couldn't help myself and included a third in my version – the guilty third fabric was simply too beautiful not to use. However, the measurements given below are for two fabrics so you can keep it simple. You can, of course, adjust this if you would like to include a third (or fourth) fabric:
Fabric 1 (pink): 3m.
Fabric 2 (cream): 4.3m – the design works best if this fabric is plain.

Due to the shape of the templates required for this design, there will be wastage when you cut the fabric, but you can use the excess for the backing, binding or other projects.

I used two plain khadi cottons – an elegant pale dusky rose and a cream. I then noticed that in my stash of vintage textiles I had a rather beautiful embroidered silk sari, lemony cream in colour with stunning embroidery. I decided to set in a few pieces to add texture and luxury against the hand-woven cotton. It works because it is tonally correct with the other fabrics and is a subtle delight rather than a bold statement. I have to say, it is a really beautiful quilt up close and personal.

QUILT BACKING

You will need approximately 5.5m of fabric. The finished size should be at least 240 x 240cm, so you can use the leftovers from the quilt top or any other fabric you choose.

I pieced together the backing for my quilt using the remainder of a sandwashed silk sari and a selection of cotton remnants.

BINDING

You will need approximately 0.5m of fabric. You can use scraps from the quilt top, or use the binding as a chance to introduce a new fabric.

I used the pale rose khadi cotton, to ensure the binding didn't compete with the quilt design.

OTHER MATERIALS

WADDING of your choice, 240 x 240cm.
SEWING THREAD 100 per cent cotton all-purpose thread is best, in a neutral colour.
QUILTING THREAD 100 per cent cotton quilting thread in a colour of your choice.

CUT YOUR FABRIC

Download patterns A and B from my website (www. cassandraellis.co.uk/worldofquilts) and print them out. Join the pieces together, cut out the pattern shapes and then trace around them onto a sheet of cardboard or thick art paper (you will need a sheet of A1 for each pattern). Transfer the two centre marks onto the card pattern.

Press fabric 1 so that it is wrinkle-free. Place it on your cutting table or on a thread-free floor. Using tailor's chalk or a pencil, trace pattern A 12 times onto the length of cloth. Transfer the centre mark onto each piece. Use the fabric efficiently by twisting the pattern piece around to fill in the gaps (but don't cut on the bias).

Then trace pattern B four times onto fabric 1, ensuring that you transfer the centre marks.

Using sharp fabric scissors, cut out all 16 pieces, making sure to cut around the curves, not into them. Clip 5mm into all the centre marks, then set the pieces aside.

Press fabric 2 and place it on your cutting table or the floor. Trace pattern A four times and pattern B 12 times. Transfer the centre marks. Cut out the 16 pieces, clip into the centre marks, then set them aside.

SEW YOUR QUILT TOP

You need to make 16 squares in total.

With right sides together, pin one of pattern A to one of pattern B, with the convex piece on top of the concave one. Make sure that you pair alternate fabrics. Match and pin the centre marks first, then pin the corners. Pin every 10mm, taking care to match the seamlines. Stitch along the curve without stretching or pulling, removing the pins as you sew. Press the seam towards the larger piece – it should lie flat without being clipped. Trim any loose threads.

Make a further 15 squares in the same way.

Use the diagram as a guide and lay your squares out in the correct order. If you have used a third (or fourth) fabric, you may want to move the squares around to get a layout that you are happy with.

Sew the four squares of the first row together, keeping your stitching precise – this will matter when you join the rows together. Press the seams open and trim away any loose threads. Repeat for the following three rows.

Pin and sew the first two rows together, matching the seams carefully. Join the remaining rows in the same way. Press all the seams and trim off any excess sewing thread.

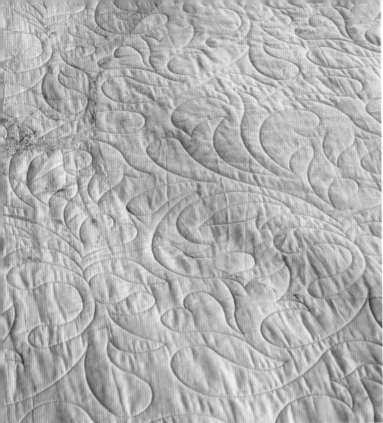

SEW YOUR QUILT BACKING

Your quilt backing needs to be a minimum of 240 x 240cm. Use the excess fabric from your quilt top or introduce something new. Join your choice of fabric together until you have a backing the right size. Press all the seams and trim away any excess threads.

BUILD YOUR QUILT

Put your quilt sandwich together in your preferred way (see page 182). After you have marked any necessary quilting lines, machine- or hand-quilt using your favourite technique (see page 184). Trim the backing and wadding so that the edges are even and your quilt is square. Finally, make and attach the binding (see page 186).

'To produce a clearly defined pattern, it is essential to match your seamlines precisely as you join each curve and row.'

MAKE IT YOURS

This quilt design is all about the fabrics, so take your time to select the perfect pair or trio to bring this fairly dramatic design to life.

RAIL FENCE

AMERICAN QUILT DESIGNS were initially based on the quilts tucked inside the trunks of the first migrants. Welsh and North Country Wholecloth and Frame quilts were made in the hundreds, if not thousands, but the designs had to be adjusted to fit the economies of the settlers' new lives. Fabric was expensive and difficult to come by, and life was hard, so the women had to find a new style of quilt-making. The original designs evolved into quilts made from blocks – and small blocks at that. Blocks were easy to work with, faster to piece and portable, all of which was important in new rural communities. Squares, triangles, strips and scraps were all used to create hundreds of new designs that reflected the landscape and environment in which the families lived.

The grid on which these quilts are created describes the blocks' design: a nine-patch block is three by three, and a four-patch block is two by two. Each block could be a number of shapes and this created an almost inexhaustible list of potential quilt designs. The Rail Fence quilt can be a three- or four-patch design, depending on whether the sewer uses three or four strips in her composition. The design was sometimes called Roman Stripe or Basketweave and was an incredibly simple quilt to cut and piece. It was originally fashioned in red, white and blue to reflect its American heritage, but now it is often made in any colour combination. As the design is so simple to make, Rail Fence blocks were often used to teach children the basics of quilting. The Amish and Gee's Bend quilters have always used the Rail Fence design, probably due to its graphic and simple nature.

Although it is hard to find any definitive history on early quilt patterns, it is often written that this design comes from the structure of an actual fence. Fences were part of the new landscape, so why not create a quilt design from it? When piecing, each block is turned in alternate directions so that each colour appears to make a stepped-fence pattern across the quilt top. Some research also suggests it was a key quilt design in the Underground Railroad movement for slaves escaping to the free states: if the Rail Fence quilt was on display, slaves knew that they were on the right path. Whether this is true or not, I think it is a comforting thought that such an effort could have been made.

Although it would have been very simple to create a whole Rail Fence quilt, I liked the idea of celebrating the concept of what it represented, and almost framing it. I looked at a great number of Gee's Bend quilts and loved how the Rail Fence blocks had often just been set within much larger pieces of cloth. By using special fabrics for the strips, I think the design is suitably elevated. Simple is often more striking than complex.

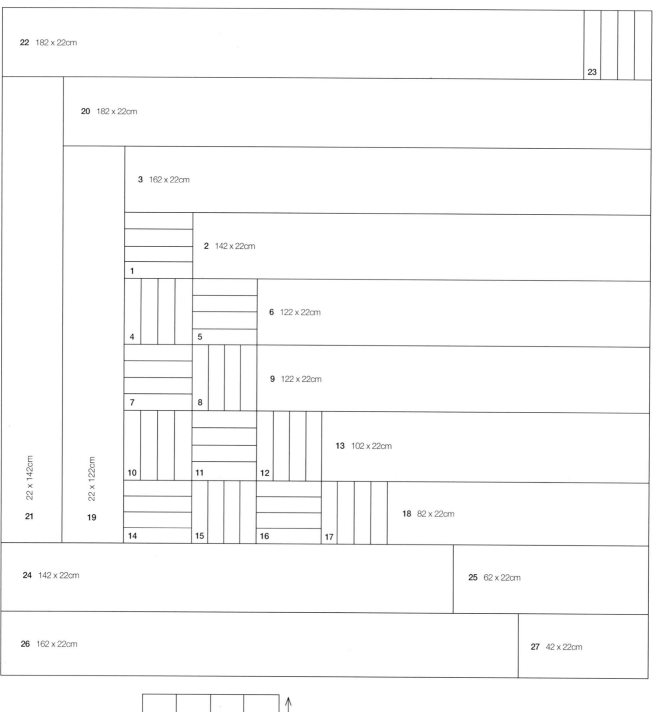

22 182 x 22cm

23

20 182 x 22cm

3 162 x 22cm

2 142 x 22cm

1

6 122 x 22cm

4

5

9 122 x 22cm

7

8

13 102 x 22cm

10

11

12

22 x 142cm

22 x 122cm

18 82 x 22cm

21

19

14

15

16

17

24 142 x 22cm

25 62 x 22cm

26 162 x 22cm

27 42 x 22cm

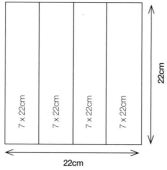

7 x 22cm
7 x 22cm
7 x 22cm
7 x 22cm

22cm

22cm

'Sometimes simple is the most striking: the Rail Fence blocks look stunning framed within large pieces of plain cloth.'

QUILT SIZE

200 x 200cm when trimmed and bound. All seam allowances are 1cm and are included in the cutting sizes.

QUILT TOP

You will need approximately 3m of fabric A and 2m of fabric B. You will also need approximately 1m of assorted remnants to make the Rail Fence blocks.

I used tactile khadi cottons for my two main fabrics – in sunny butter (A) and pale ivory (B) – delicious! I then gathered an assortment of silk scraps in yellow, coffee, red and pink for the Rail Fence blocks. I think it is most definitely a cheerful quilt, but it is also surprisingly calm.

Simple to piece together, this is a wonderful quilt design for framing precious cloth, and it works well as either an adult's or a child's quilt.

QUILT BACKING

You will need approximately 5m of fabric. The finished size should be at least 220 x 220cm. You can use leftovers from your quilt top to make the backing, a sheet or sari, as well as fabric from a bolt of cloth.

I went a bit crazy choosing the backing fabrics for this quilt. I had recently visited Great Dixter house and gardens in Northiam, East Sussex, and loved the riotous borders of flowers that were laid out in contrasting rows. Using this idea, I pieced the backing in vertical strips in a mixture of Japanese silks and Indian cottons in smoky purple, yellow, pink and taupe.

BINDING

You will need approximately 0.5m of fabric. You can use scraps from the quilt top if you have any left over, or use the binding as an opportunity to introduce a new fabric.

I used strips of the butter khadi to tie the whole quilt together.

OTHER MATERIALS

WADDING of your choice, 220 x 220cm.
SEWING THREAD 100 per cent cotton all-purpose thread is best, in a neutral colour.
QUILTING THREAD 100 per cent cotton quilting thread in a colour of your choice.

CUT YOUR FABRIC

Start by cutting your Rail Fence strips. You need to cut 52 strips measuring 7 x 22cm. You can use any number of fabrics if you want to randomly piece these blocks together. Alternatively, you can use just four different fabrics and sew each block identically. You will need to cut 13 strips in each fabric for this method.

To cut fabric A, cut continuous strips 22cm wide. (You should have four strips per standard width of fabric; if you have selected a wide fabric, you should be able to cut five strips.) Then cut the following:
2 of 182 x 22cm (pieces 20 and 22)
1 of 162 x 22cm (piece 3)
1 of 142 x 22cm (piece 2)
2 of 122 x 22cm (pieces 6 and 9)
1 of 102 x 22cm (piece 13)
1 of 82 x 22cm (piece 18)
1 of 62 x 22cm (piece 25)
1 of 42 x 22cm (piece 22)
You may need to join pieces together to get the required lengths, but try to pair a short piece with a long piece to avoid too many seams – 182cm and 102cm can be cut easily from a 3m length with little wastage. Mark the length on the back in tailor's chalk or pencil to avoid confusion later.

Repeat the process with fabric B. Cut 22cm strips from your width of fabric and cut the following:
1 of 162 x 22cm (piece 26)
2 of 142 x 22cm (pieces 21 and 24)
1 of 122 x 22cm (piece 19)

SEW YOUR QUILT TOP

Start by piecing your Rail Fence blocks together. Choose four pieces from your cut pile and sew them together in an order that you are happy with. Press the seams and trim away any loose threads. Repeat for the remaining 12 blocks. Press all the blocks and make sure they are 22cm square. You can cut away any excess or straighten up any lines with your rotary cutter and mat if need be. You are ready to piece the whole quilt top together.

If your Rail Fence squares have the same fabric combinations, the quilt top is straightforward to sew. If you have used different fabric combinations, you may want to preplan which block goes where. Take a picture or two, to remind yourself of your favourite compositions.

Follow the diagram on page 24 and piece the quilt top together in number order. Alternate the direction of the Rail Fence blocks and pin the long pieces together before sewing to avoid them twisting and stretching. Press the seams as you go and trim loose threads. Once you have sewn all 27 pieces together, your quilt top is complete.

SEW YOUR QUILT BACKING

Your quilt backing needs to be a minimum of 220 x 220cm. You may have fabric that is already that size. If not, simply join your choice of fabric until you have a backing the right size. This can be in strips, squares or 'freestyling'. Press all the seams and trim away any excess threads. Your quilt backing is complete.

BUILD YOUR QUILT

Put your quilt sandwich together in your preferred way (see page 182). After you have marked any necessary quilting lines, machine- or hand-quilt using your favourite technique (see page 184). Trim the backing and wadding so that the edges are even and your quilt is square. Finally, make and attach the binding (see page 186).

'This quilt is wonderful for framing precious cloth, and the strips of silk in yellow, coffee, red and pink elevate the simple design.'

MAKE IT YOURS

This is such a simple quilt to piece and is striking when finished. Take your time to find the right fabrics, as they really are the stars. This isn't a quilt you can easily make smaller, but you can make it larger by adding two extra strips. Instead of Rail Fence blocks, you could create String or Gee's Bend blocks – or a combination of all of them.

KANTHA

THE KANTHA IS another quilt born of poverty, yet an object of utter beauty. The word Kantha comes from the Sanskrit *kontha*, which means rags. Historically, making Kantha from rags was essential within the folk belief ideals prevalent in India. The use of scraps and worn-out fabric created a sense of unity within the finished piece, by demonstrating that there was real beauty in old things. The first Kantha were recorded more than 500 years ago, so the concept of recycling, or up-cycling, is far from new. Kantha have been made by both Hindu and Muslim women, and different traditions are evident within the textile because of their diverse beliefs. However, the folk belief system surrounding Kantha was stronger, and the construction, cloth and symbolism of stitching unified the individual faiths.

The earliest and simplest form of Kantha was the patchwork Nakshi Kantha, which are still made for children or as simple throws and blankets. It is often the quilt style we associate with Kantha and was one of my first quilt loves. The Kantha evolved from this into a highly decorative embroidered piece with extensive motifs adorning the fabric. Large Kantha were used as quilts and ground covers, while smaller pieces were used as book covers, cushions and bags. These embroidered pieces have become a great source of pride to the Bangladeshi people and are highly sought-after.

Kantha were originally made from worn-out saris and dhotis – the traditional clothing for Bangladeshi men and women. The cloth was softened and made colourfast from years of washing, which made the fabric easy to sew through and functional as household goods. Threads were pulled from the woven borders of the sari cloth and used as the embroidery and quilting thread. The layers of cloth were spread flat on the ground and held in place with weights at the edges. They were then sewn together with rows of large tacking stitches. The cloth was then folded and worked on whenever there was time – it could take years for a woman to finish one piece of Kantha if everyday living got in the way. As with many of the quilt cultures in this book, the women sat on the ground with just a needle and thread to create these works of art – no hoops, tools or frames were necessary.

My version of this great tradition is to honour my favourite patchwork Nakshi Kantha. Old fabrics, simply pieced, with decorative stitching – this is a quilt style I have loved for a long time and one that I will continue to make.

QUILT SIZE

210 x 210cm when trimmed and bound. All seam allowances are 1cm and are already built into the cutting sizes.

QUILT TOP

You will need approximately 5–7m of fabric. This quilt top is made by piecing fabric together without a preplanned design or set of measurements. The quantity of fabric you need depends on the fabric you already have, what you purchase, and how many pieces you cut and sew together – using smaller pieces means more seams, which means more fabric.

I have used my beloved Japanese kimono silk for this quilt. As well as being my favourite cloth, it is perfect for creating a Kantha-style quilt. (To find places to buy kimono silk, see Resources, page 190.)

QUILT BACKING

You will need approximately 5m of fabric. The finished size should be at least 230 x 230cm. You could use the left-over fabric from the front, or contrast the busy nature of this quilt with a plain backing – it is up to you.

I used some plain khadi cotton from my fabric stash to make the backing for this quilt.

BINDING

You will need approximately 0.5m of fabric. You can use scraps from the quilt top if you have any left over, or use the binding as an opportunity to introduce a new fabric.

I used an ivory habotai silk that I have used in the body of several other quilts, because I wanted the quilt to have a silky, tactile sensation from top to toe.

OTHER MATERIALS

WADDING of your choice, 230 x 230cm.
SEWING THREAD 100 per cent cotton all-purpose thread is best, in a neutral colour.
QUILTING THREAD 100 per cent cotton quilting thread in a colour of your choice.

CUT AND SEW YOUR FABRIC

This quilt is different from the others in that there is no diagram or set piecing pattern. You will plan, piece, sew and trim all at once. It works along the same principle as the Gee's Bend quilt (see page 34), but on a much larger scale. You are building blocks, as for all other quilts, but with no predetermined pattern or measurements. This quilt does require a considerable block of time to put it together – mostly for the planning, rather than the sewing – so try to put aside at least 3–4 hours. Sounds like heaven…

Gather all your fabric and lay it out on a queen-size bed, or larger, or a clear floor space (make sure this is spotless). If you can, chalk or mark with pins a square measuring at least 215 x 215cm. Pull out the fabrics that you want to use as a feature in your quilt – it might be the colour or the pattern that you want to highlight, or both. Position them roughly where you would like them to be in the design and then place other fabrics around them to create a balanced composition. Keep moving pieces around until you have a layout you are really happy with. Use your camera, phone or tablet to record different ideas.

In order to sew this quilt together, you need to 'build blocks'. Most of the other quilt projects in the book use this idea as their basis. For this quilt, you are simply cutting and joining pieces together to create larger pieces using the same method – the only difference with this project is that you are freestyling without a diagram to follow. When joining two pieces together, both have to be the same length (or width) after you have sewn them together and before you can join another piece. For example, if one piece is longer than the other, you will need to trim off any excess before you join the next piece.

Once you have a layout you are happy with, it is time to start sewing.

SEW YOUR QUILT TOP

Start from one edge of your quilt and work across or down. You will need to create several smaller blocks, before you piece the whole quilt. Look at the Housetop, Utility and Boro quilt designs (see pages 66, 88 and 100) to remind yourself how this works.

Pin and sew two pieces together. Press the seams and trim loose threads. If one piece is longer or wider than the other, trim off any excess before you join the next piece. Continue cutting and joining pieces, following your layout. You may find that you need to add extra pieces or reduce pieces from your original layout – just take your time.

Finished quilt top measures: 212 x 212cm

'Japanese kimono silk, with its vibrant colour palettes and painterly designs, is not only my favourite cloth, but is also perfect for creating a Kantha quilt.'

Once you have reached the required size, press well, remove excess threads and trim the quilt top to make sure it is the right size and also square.

SEW YOUR QUILT BACKING

Your quilt backing needs to be a minimum of 230 x 230cm. Join your choice of fabric together until you have a backing the right size. Press all the seams and trim away any excess threads. Your quilt backing is now complete.

BUILD YOUR QUILT

Put your quilt sandwich together in your preferred way (see page 182). After you have marked any necessary quilting lines, machine- or hand-quilt using your favourite technique (see page 184). Trim the backing and wadding so that the edges are even and your quilt is square. Finally, make and attach the binding (see page 186).

MAKE IT YOURS

This design is all about you to begin with. Remember, you can make the quilt any size. Combine this freestyle technique with the Gee's Bend quilt ideas (see page 34) to create wonderful cot or lap quilts. They will be fast, stunning and very personal.

GEE'S BEND

WHY IS IT that so many of the most beautiful quilts are created from lives of poverty, restriction and isolation? Perhaps the restraint focused the makers' creativity, so that it became a haven away from the day-to-day grind. The quilts of Gee's Bend are probably the most striking and moving quilts of them all – to me, at least. They are often wonky, with no pattern or preplanned fabric placement – a far cry from the ordered regularity of other quilt groups. The colour combinations are bold, bordering on riotous, and are mixed with no care for strict colour-wheel guidelines. The fabrics are old, and different weights, compositions and textures are mixed together – a no-no for some. And yet they are a glorious illustration of the power of resourcefulness.

Gee's Bend is a hamlet in Wilcox County, Alabama, on a remote peninsula on the Alabama River. The community is mostly descended from slaves and has known more than its fair share of crippling poverty and hardship. The hamlet was named after Joseph Gee, the first white man to stake a land claim in the area. In time, the Gee family sold their cotton plantation and their 47 slaves to the Pettways, and many of today's Gee's Bend quilters still carry the surname Pettway. The female slaves on the plantation created quilts from whatever materials were available – the closest settlement was almost unreachable and there were no resources apart from their old clothes. Their homes were mere shacks, with no running water or electricity, so Gee's Bend women made quilts to keep themselves and their children warm – their quilts were almost all they had. As time passed, they developed the idiosyncratic style we know and love as a Gee's Bend quilt.

Even after freedom came, life continued to be difficult. During the early 1930s all their food, seed, animals and tools were taken away by debt collectors. They relied on the Red Cross to provide food and rations, but can you imagine losing your possessions when you had only recently been given the right to own at all? The land was eventually sold to the government, which created a co-operative scheme, allowing the families to farm and own their land. They lived through the Depression, catastrophic flooding and political unrest – and still they created these amazing quilts.

While each quilt-maker has her unique aesthetic, the community collectively has created something very important from both an arts and an anthropological point of view. The women of Gee's Bend have passed their skills and creativity down through at least six generations, and although there are only around 50 current members, their strength, resilience and originality should inspire all of us to create the best quilt versions of ourselves and our lives.

My version was a joy to plan and piece. There is structure to the design, but I hope you will let yourself run free with the central blocks, as I did. It is a truly liberating form of quilt-making.

Finished quilt top measures: 212 x 212cm

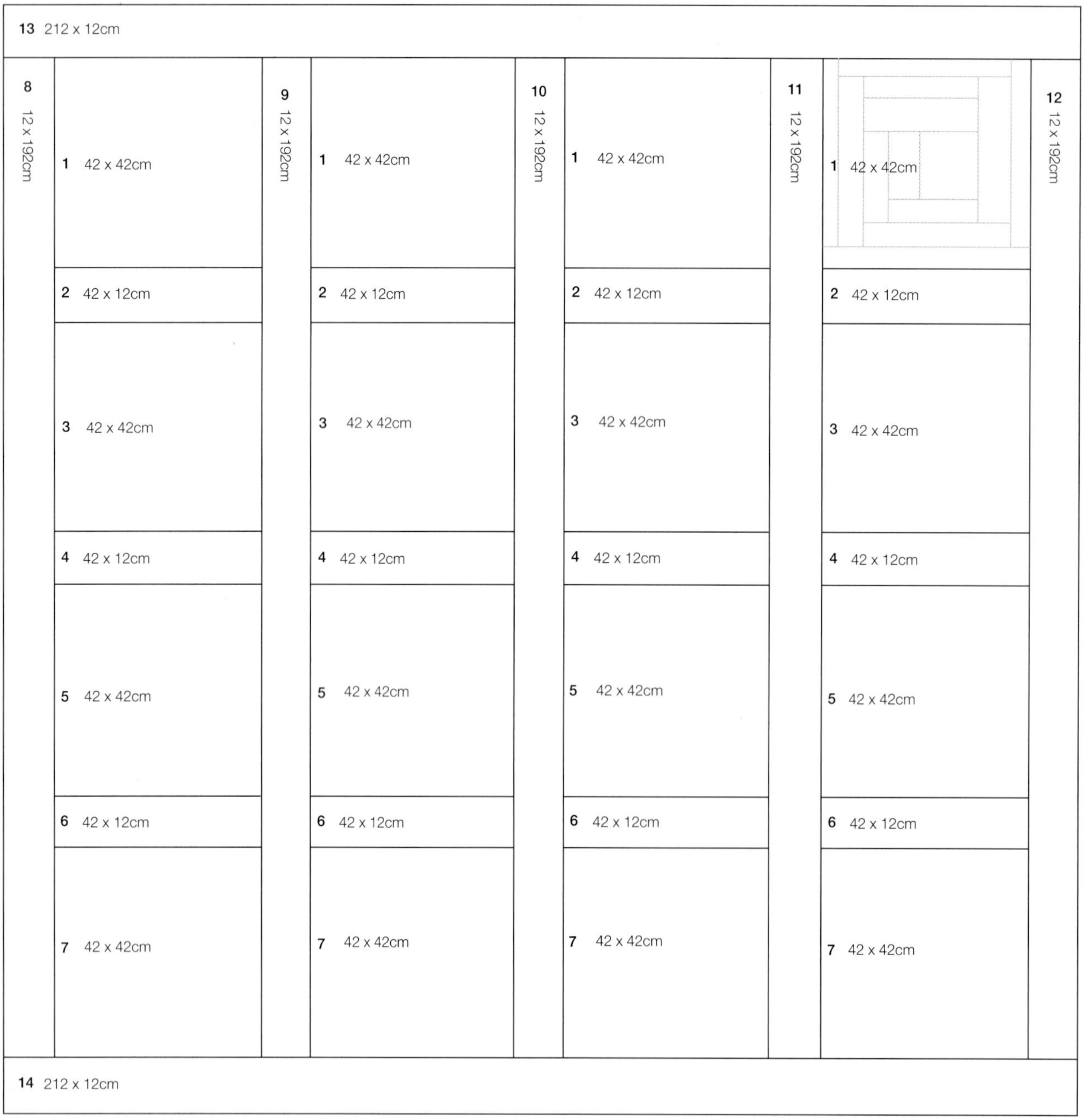
13 212 x 12cm
8 12 x 192cm
1 42 x 42cm
2 42 x 12cm
3 42 x 42cm
4 42 x 12cm
5 42 x 42cm
6 42 x 12cm
7 42 x 42cm
9 12 x 192cm
1 42 x 42cm
2 42 x 12cm
3 42 x 42cm
4 42 x 12cm
5 42 x 42cm
6 42 x 12cm
7 42 x 42cm
10 12 x 192cm
1 42 x 42cm
2 42 x 12cm
3 42 x 42cm
4 42 x 12cm
5 42 x 42cm
6 42 x 12cm
7 42 x 42cm
11 12 x 192cm
1 42 x 42cm
2 42 x 12cm
3 42 x 42cm
4 42 x 12cm
5 42 x 42cm
6 42 x 12cm
7 42 x 42cm
12 12 x 192cm
14 212 x 12cm

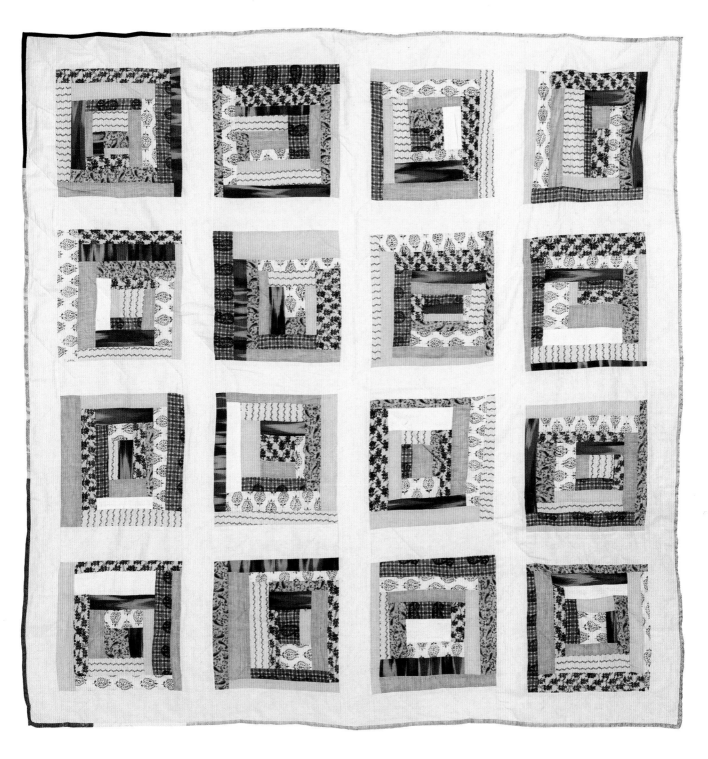

'Both striking and moving, Gee's Bend quilts are a glorious illustration of the power of resourcefulness.'

QUILT SIZE

210 x 210cm when trimmed and bound. All seam allowances are 1cm and are already built into the cutting sizes.

QUILT TOP

You will need approximately 2.2m of your border fabric and 3–4m of fabric for your freestyle centre blocks, which are based on a Log Cabin design (see page 132). You can use lots of scraps with this method or buy yardage specifically for this quilt. Your border fabric needs to be a medium-weight cotton or linen, while your centre blocks can be a mixture of any fabric you like.

I used my favourite plain ivory khadi cotton for the border and a wonderful mixture of block-printed and woven Indian cottons for the freestyle blocks. (Look at the Resources on page 190 for great suppliers of Indian cottons.)

QUILT BACKING

You will need approximately 5m of fabric. The finished size should be at least 230 x 230cm, so you can use fabric leftovers to make the backing, or fabric from a bolt of cloth.

I used the remainder of my ivory khadi cotton, mixed with two different vintage silk saris. I had used the heavily patterned part of the saris for the front of another quilt, so the left-over simpler silk was perfect for a backing.

BINDING

You will need approximately 0.5m of fabric. You can use scraps from the quilt top if you have any left over, or use the binding as an opportunity to introduce a new fabric.

I used the khadi cotton so that the edging was barely discernible from the borders.

OTHER MATERIALS

WADDING of your choice, 230 x 230cm.
SEWING THREAD 100 per cent cotton all-purpose thread is best, in a neutral colour.
QUILTING THREAD 100 per cent cotton quilting thread in a colour of your choice.

CUT YOUR FABRIC

Cut your border fabric first. Cut 12cm strips running the length of the piece of fabric – 2.2m. Then cut these strips into the following:

12 of 12 x 42cm (pieces 2, 4 and 6, x 4)
5 of 12 x 192cm (pieces 8, 9, 10, 11 and 12)
2 of 12 x 212cm (pieces 13 and 14)

You will have some fabric left over (unless you have used narrow fabric), but you can use this for your binding, backing or other projects.

Your centre blocks will be cut and sewn at the same time, so you are ready to start piecing.

SEW YOUR QUILT TOP

This is the kind of quilt-making I love – no pattern per se, but a rough idea of what you are trying to make and the complete freedom to put together colours and shapes that you find beautiful. The centre blocks are based on the idea of a Log Cabin, but without measurements or a predetermined direction of placement.

Start by lining up all your fabrics in individual piles near your cutting area. Choose your first fabric and cut a piece between 4cm and 10cm in length and any width. Choose a second piece of fabric and cut that roughly the same length as the first piece. For example, if you cut your first piece 6 x 11cm, your second piece could be 11 x 9cm. You don't actually have to measure them, but start with a smallish piece in your centre. Sew the first two pieces together and press. Trim off any excess if one piece is longer than the other. Then pick another fabric and cut a third piece that roughly fits one of the lengths of your block. Sew, press and trim. Spin the growing block around so that you are creating a loose Log Cabin. You can include angled pieces if you wish and use your eye to create a good composition. Keep going until you have a block that measures at least 43 x 43cm. Press well and trim it down to a square measuring 42 x 42cm. That is one block complete (and possibly a change in your quilt-making style forever).

Make 15 more blocks using the same method, and then you are ready to piece the quilt together. I found each block took a couple of hours, but you can get into a speedy rhythm if you have a day to spare. Otherwise, it is an easy quilt to pick up and put down.

To piece the whole quilt together, look at the diagram on page 36. You need to create four vertical rows of four blocks interspersed with the border fabric. You may want to plan where each block will be placed, so lay them down, spin them around and create a composition that you like the look of. If you have used a special fabric in the blocks, make sure that it is balanced across the whole quilt. Remember to use your phone, camera or tablet to record possible layouts.

To create the first row, sew all seven pieces together in the order of the diagram. Press the seams and trim loose threads. Repeat with the remaining three rows.

Then join border 8 to your first row. Press the seams. Join border 9 to the other edge of your first row. Press the seams. Continue adding rows and borders until you have added border 12, making sure that your rows and seams are lining up in both directions. Finally, join borders 13 and 14 to the remaining edges. Press again, trim away loose threads, and your quilt top is complete.

SEW YOUR QUILT BACKING

Your quilt backing needs to be a minimum of 230 x 230cm. Join your choice of fabric together until you have a backing the right size. Press all the seams and trim away any excess threads. Your quilt backing is now complete.

BUILD YOUR QUILT

Put your quilt sandwich together in your preferred way (see page 182). After you have marked any necessary quilting lines, machine- or hand-quilt using your favourite technique (see page 184). Trim the backing and wadding so that the edges are even and your quilt is square. Finally, make and attach the binding (see page 186).

MAKE IT YOURS

What can't you do to this quilt to make it yours? Remove the borders, increase the size of the centre blocks, or increase or reduce the size of the quilt overall by adding more or fewer rows and borders. The choice really is yours.

WILD GOOSE CHASE

THE HISTORY OF America can be told through the history of quilt designs. Pioneering American women created thousands of quilt blocks and patterns that reflected their day-to-day lives. Designs from the homeland were no longer relevant or possible to re-create in their new environment. The terrain on which they lived, as well as the sky and landscape surrounding them, informed their new designs. The gardens they created and the communities they founded were also integral to this progression. Last but not least were the battles and rules of their new culture. Often the only way of expressing their thoughts and beliefs was through their hands.

Nature was an obvious and rich source of quilt patterns for women. Infrastructure was minimal, so families often lived in isolation with only Mother Nature as a neighbour. There are many patterns named for trees, flowers, animals and birds, and Flying Geese, or Wild Goose Chase, is one of the most popular. Geese migrated twice yearly to and from Canada, across most of America; it isn't hard to imagine a quilt design being born of this amazing sight. Triangles are a simple geometric shape that are used to make hundreds of different quilt patterns. A basic (and very simple) Flying Geese block consists of one large triangle (the goose) flanked by two smaller triangles (the sky). Fabrics needed to be contrasting in tone so that the birds stood out from the sky. Women expressed their artistic abilities and creativity in the way they arranged the triangles or geese, and in the colours they used. They could be 'flying' in any formation, and there are more than a dozen different geese quilt block designs.

Flying Geese is also said to be one of the key quilts of the Underground Railroad movement, along with Drunkard's Path and Log Cabin (see pages 16 and 132). Each quilt had a specific code attached to it, and this quilt pattern told the fleeing slaves to follow the birds and travel north to the free states.

Perhaps because I am a lover of gardens and nature, I like the idea of this quilt design very much. I love to watch birds fly in flocks, especially if I catch the moment when they break away and re-form. It is quite magical and strangely moving. So my design is based on this moment – a flock flying together, but separated momentarily before they continue forward as a flock again. It is a lovely parallel to family life, which I think makes this quilt a wonderful gift or tribute to someone special.

Finished quilt top measures: 222 x 222cm

CUT YOUR FABRIC
From your main fabric cut the following, cutting your large pieces first:
6 of 22 x 72cm
4 of 22 x 62cm
2 of 22 x 52cm
4 of 22 x 32cm
286 of 12 x 12cm

From your support fabric(s) cut:
143 of 12 x 22cm

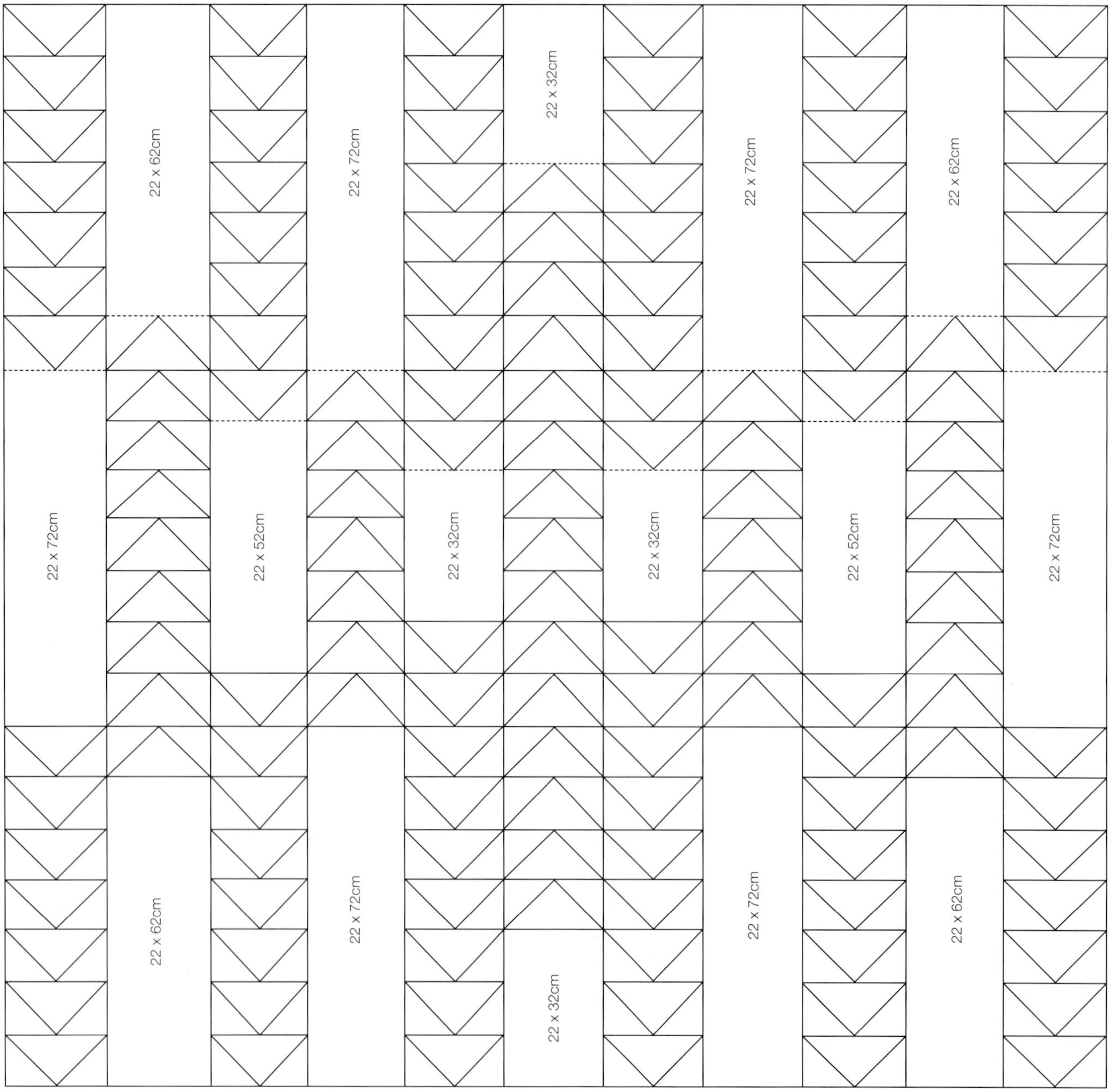

'The basic block consists
of one large triangle
(the goose) flanked by two
smaller ones (the sky).'

QUILT SIZE
220 x 220cm when trimmed and bound. All seam allowances are 1cm and are already built into the cutting sizes.

QUILT TOP
You will need approximately 6m of your main fabric and 3.5m of your support fabric (your geese). You can use just two fabrics for the whole quilt, or you can add a third or fourth fabric if you want to create a family of 'geese'. Look at the photograph on page 43 to give you an idea for placement if you want to use more than two fabrics.

My main two fabrics are, of course, my beloved khadi cottons – in ivory and pale grey-blue this time. For a little extra movement, I added in a piece of black kimono silk and a black block-printed French cotton. I love the softness of the two main colours punctuated by the black. It is neither feminine nor masculine and it is one of my favourite quilts – which is probably why I spent more than 60 hours hand-quilting it.

QUILT BACKING
You will need approximately 5.5m of fabric. The finished size should be 240 x 240cm. You could use the left-over fabric from the front, or contrast the graphic nature of this quilt with a plain backing – it is up to you.

I used a dark blue-grey organic cotton voile for the backing to keep the quilt soft and simple.

BINDING
You will need approximately 0.5m of fabric. You can use scraps from the quilt top if you have any left over, or use the binding as an opportunity to introduce a new fabric.

I used the ivory khadi to keep it simple and ensure the quilt itself remains the focus of attention.

OTHER MATERIALS
WADDING of your choice, 240 x 240cm.
SEWING THREAD 100 per cent cotton all-purpose thread is best, in a neutral colour.
QUILTING THREAD 100 per cent cotton quilting thread in a colour of your choice.

CUT YOUR FABRIC

The quilt itself is simple to make, but it does take time to cut and piece. Make sure your rotary cutter is super-sharp and your main and support fabric are well pressed. Refer to the diagram on page 42 for cutting instructions.

SEW YOUR QUILT TOP

Start by sewing the geese. Place one 12cm square at one end of the 12 x 22cm rectangle, with right sides together. Using a pencil or tailor's chalk, draw a diagonal line across the square from corner to corner, then stitch along that line. Trim the excess off both layers at the outer corner, leaving a 1cm seam allowance, and press the remainder of the original square to form the outer triangle (the sky). Repeat with a second square on the opposite end of the rectangle, ensuring you draw the diagonal line in the correct direction (the new square will slightly overlap the previous piece). You will have some wastage from this method, but the simplicity of this piecing style far outweighs the excess scrap. Repeat until you have made 143 geese blocks. Before piecing them together, trim off any 'tails'. Re-measure and square up your blocks to be accurate (each should measure 12 x 22cm).

Following the diagram on page 42, sew the correct number of geese blocks together. For example, for the first row you need to make two blocks of seven geese. Continue piecing until you have sewn all 17 geese blocks together. Press the blocks and trim off excess threads.

Piece the quilt top row by row, following the diagram to ensure you join the correct plain blocks to geese blocks. Once you have assembled all 11 rows, pin and sew the rows together, being careful not to stretch or twist them. Press the seams and trim any threads.

SEW YOUR QUILT BACKING

The quilt backing needs to be a minimum of 240 x 240cm. Join together your choice of fabric until you have a backing the right size. Press the seams and trim any threads.

BUILD YOUR QUILT

Assemble your quilt sandwich in your preferred way (see page 182). Mark any quilting lines and machine- or hand-quilt using your favourite technique (see page 184). Trim the backing and wadding so that the edges are even and square. Finally, make and attach the binding (see page 186).

'It isn't hard to imagine a quilt design being born of the amazing sight of flocks of geese migrating.'

MAKE IT YOURS

Although time-consuming to make, this is a very easy quilt to personalize. The 'geese' can be any number and combination of colours, and it is simple to increase or reduce the size of the quilt. This is an excellent quilt for children – either as a memory blanket or as a storyteller if you choose the right fabrics.

SWEDISH

AS WAS THE CASE in many countries and cultures, Swedish quilts were first made for the rich and noble before quilt-making became a necessity for the poor. Usually created from silk, wool cloth and felt, fifteenth-century quilts were a luxury for the very wealthy. Heavily stitched and appliquéd, they were considered to be pieces of art as well as functional objects, and were found only in the homes of the nobility or within church walls; commoners made do with animal hides or rag rugs as bed covers. Fabric was far too expensive to be used for anything other than clothes, and laws demanded that all linen rags were sent to paper mills for the manufacture of money, ensuring a constant shortfall of fabric for poor families for more than a hundred years.

Imported cotton appeared in Sweden around 1870 and it was then used alongside any left-over wool, silk or linen to create quilts. Fabric could be bought from dry goods stores, travelling salesmen or the local seamstress, who would sell left-over scraps to housewives. Worn-out clothes were recycled and quilt backs were made from a flax yarn that had been roughly hand-spun. If the quilt-maker was lucky, the wadding would be made from wool; if not, from linen scraps, rags or even paper mixed with animal hair. Quilts were often very simple in style, narrow in width, and made by both men and women.

As cotton became cheaper, quilt-making became more popular. In much of Sweden, the possession of large numbers of perfectly made quilts established the housewife's thrift and sewing skills, as well as the family's standing in society.

Some say the biggest influence on Swedish quilts came from America. At the same time as quilting became popular, Swedish families were moving back from the New World to their homeland. Living conditions had improved significantly in Sweden, so those who had originally moved to America for a better life, returned home. They brought American quilting styles back with them, and magazines offered American patterns written specifically for Swedish women. After the First World War, quilting began to disappear as handmade goods became a sign of poverty.

Swedish quilts are often thought of as something that was necessary in a family's day-to-day life, but were not an 'art' that defined Swedish culture. Many of the old Swedish quilts I have seen are charming in a naïve and cheerful manner, so perhaps functionality was enough. They are optimistic and not overly complicated, which is what I love about them. My version is based on a style of quilt from the 1870s. It is extremely simple in construction and fabric choice, as I wanted to reflect what I believe makes these quilts unique from all others.

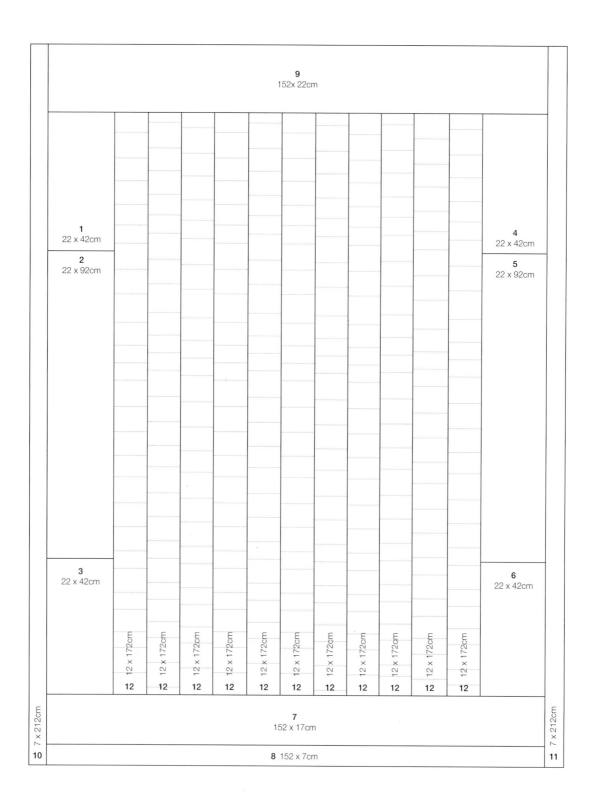

9
152x 22cm

1
22 x 42cm

4
22 x 42cm

2
22 x 92cm

5
22 x 92cm

3
22 x 42cm

6
22 x 42cm

12 x 172cm
12

12 x 172cm
12

12 x 172cm
12

12 x 172cm
12

12 x 172cm
12

12 x 172cm
12

12 x 172cm
12

12 x 172cm
12

12 x 172cm
12

12 x 172cm
12

12 x 172cm
12

7 x 212cm

7 x 212cm

7
152 x 17cm

10

8 152 x 7cm

11

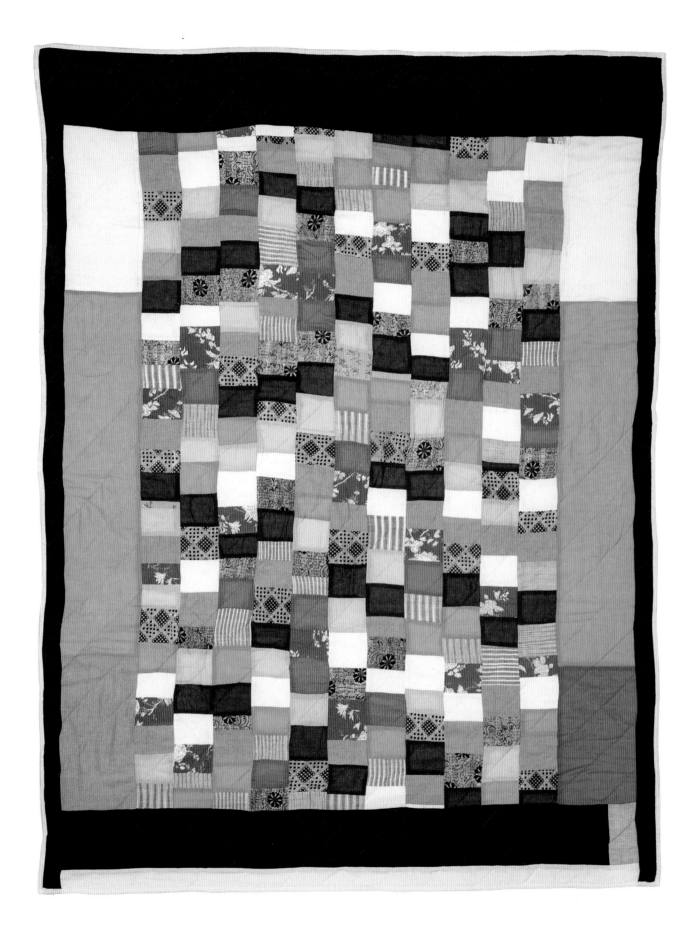

QUILT SIZE

160 x 210cm when trimmed and bound. All seam allowances are 1cm and are included in the cutting sizes.

QUILT TOP

You will need approximately 4–5m of fabric. The middle section of the quilt can be made of scraps (in keeping with the spirit of the quilt), or you can select new fabrics to fit with the border cloth. The longest piece of fabric you will need is 212cm, but you can join pieces together to create this length if necessary – I added a contrasting piece to one end of block 7. This type of quilt was always about making beauty out of very little, so rummage through your cupboards and wardrobes to pull something together.

I chose a warm but subtle colour palette and selected 12–15 different fabrics. Some were fragments or fat quarters and others were pieces over 1m in length. I used a mixture of plain cotton and linen, alongside block-printed and woven French and Indian cotton prints. I chose relatively small-scale prints because I wanted this quilt to be modest and comforting.

QUILT BACKING

You will need approximately 4m of fabric. The finished size should be at least 180 x 230cm, so you can piece together left-over cloth or any other soft cotton to make the backing.

BINDING

You will need approximately 0.5m of fabric. You can use left-over scraps from the quilt top, or use the binding as an opportunity to introduce a new fabric.

I used a mixture of ivory cotton and scraps to keep it simple.

OTHER MATERIALS

WADDING of your choice, 180 x 230cm.
SEWING THREAD 100 per cent cotton all-purpose thread is best, in a neutral colour.
QUILTING THREAD 100 per cent cotton quilting thread in a colour of your choice.

CUT YOUR FABRIC

This is a very easy quilt to cut and piece, as the design is just 11 randomly pieced strips, surrounded by a simple border. Once you have measured and cut the border pieces, you can spend short bursts of time cutting the remainder and piecing it all together. It is the perfect project to start your quilt-making journey, and a very good quilt to use up fabric from other projects. I think it works particularly well as a child's quilt, as the design is fairly naïve.

Look at the diagram on page 48 and start by cutting out the border pieces. You can preplan every fabric placement before you start cutting. If you are happy to mark the diagram, then draw these in now. Otherwise, trace the diagram with tracing paper and mark your fabric choices on that. Cut out the eight 22cm-wide border pieces, mark the number on the back with pencil or tailor's chalk, and set aside. Then cut the three 7cm-wide border pieces, joining lengths together if you need to. Mark the number on the back and set aside.

Cut the remaining border fabric into 12cm-wide strips. Then cut each strip into random widths of between 4cm and 10cm. Put your cut fabric into individual piles.

Gather your remaining fabrics together and press. Select your first fabric and cut it into 12cm-wide strips – they can be any length. Using your rotary cutter and quilter's ruler, cut the fabric into irregular widths. This is one of the few quilt designs where you don't need to measure. You will find a natural rhythm and that cutting in this method is terrifically quick.

Once you have cut all of the first fabric, put it aside and cut the rest using the same technique. You may cut more or less than you need, but you can always add in more fabrics if you run out, or use the excess to start another quilt. Place each fabric into its own pile or individual envelope and you are ready to sew the quilt together.

SEW YOUR QUILT TOP

From your individual fabric piles, choose your first two pieces and sew them with right sides together. Continue adding pieces, in an order that you are happy with, until your first row is 175cm long. Don't worry about drawing evenly from each of the different fabrics – you will find an intrinsic regularity that comes naturally. Once your first row is complete, press, and trim it to 12 x 172cm. Repeat this process for the remaining ten rows.

Lay the 11 rows down side by side and move them around to create an order that you like. You can switch the direction of the rows as well as changing their order. Use your phone, camera or tablet to record different layouts. When you are happy with the configuration, pin and sew each row together, being careful not to stretch them. To ensure straight rows, simply rotate the piece 180° each time you stitch two of the rows together. Press all the seams and cut away loose threads. Your central block is complete.

Next, sew border pieces 1, 2 and 3 with right sides together in the order of the diagram on page 48. Press and set aside. Sew pieces 4, 5 and 6 in the same manner. Press and set aside. Repeat for pieces 7 and 8.

Using the diagram as a guide, pin and sew block 1/2/3 to the left edge of the central block. Pin and sew block 4/5/6 to the right edge. Press both seams. Pin and sew block 7/8 to the bottom edge of the central block. Pin and sew piece 9 to the top edge of the central block. Press the seams. Finally, pin and sew pieces 10 and 11 to each side edge. Press the seams, trim away any loose threads, and your quilt top is complete.

SEW YOUR QUILT BACKING

The quilt backing needs to be a minimum of 180 x 230cm. Sew your choice of fabric to the correct size. Press all the seams and trim away any excess threads. Your quilt backing is now complete.

BUILD YOUR QUILT

Put your quilt sandwich together in your preferred way (see page 182). After you have marked any necessary quilting lines, machine- or hand-quilt using your favourite technique (see page 184). Trim the backing and wadding so that the edges are even and your quilt is square. Finally, make and attach the binding (see page 186).

MAKE IT YOURS

This quilt design can be easily adjusted to make it larger or smaller. To increase the quilt to fit a queen-size bed, add six more strips to the central block and increase the length of pieces 7, 8 and 9 to 212cm. You will need an extra 1.5m of fabric for this size quilt. You can also adjust the widths of the rows in the centre for a simpler or busier quilt. Last but not least, you can cut the central pieces at an angle as well as straight up and down to create a different feel (see the String quilt on page 106).

NORTH COUNTRY FRAME

THE LATE NINETEENTH and early twentieth centuries are thought of as a golden age of quilt-making in Britain. North Country 'Frame' quilts were made in significant numbers during this time and were indicative of the style of quilters in the region, as well as providing a much-needed source of income. Made in the counties of Northumberland, Durham and Yorkshire, they are sometimes known simply as Durham quilts. Mining and farming were the main sources of income, and villages grew around these industries. Quilts were important both socially and economically to these communities, as life was often challenging on many levels. Families and friends would sew together at social gatherings, where they would combine quilt-making with music, singing and dancing. The quilts were revered for their beauty and quality, but they also became an essential part of the rural economy. Women would sell quilts to help support their families, often as a sideline to dressmaking.

When making a Frame quilt, quilters planned visual tension and repetition between the frames and the central medallion. Each fabric might not be used in order but would build a harmonious pattern as the quilt grew. Like other quilts from around the world, a Frame quilt wasn't necessarily preplanned. The quilter would use their eye and available fabrics to create a pleasing combination, using the central piece as their starting point. This method gave the maker freedom to create something unique. The quilt designs developed over time, becoming looser in structure, and often quilters turned to Wholecloth quilts instead, using stitching to create a central motif.

Like Welsh quilters, the North Country quilters benefited from the formation of the Rural Industries Board in 1921. To be accepted on the quilt-making scheme, they not only had to be excellent quilters, but were also means tested to see who needed the work most. However, the social and economic changes after the Second World War brought quilting to an abrupt halt.

Frame quilts are joyous to look at, which is odd considering they came from areas of extreme poverty. Why is it that beauty often comes from hardship? Perhaps the importance of family and community imbues these quilts with happiness and harmony. Perhaps it is the pride in stitching and choice of fabrics. I think it is all of these things, and I am delighted that I have been lucky enough to see yet another illustration of beauty triumphing over circumstance.

I had a great time planning this quilt. I wanted to base it on a painting of a forest floor that I had seen in a gallery. The painting was dark but tranquil and almost fractured, like shafts of light coming through trees. I also wanted to reduce the frame design to its bare bones – like stripping away layers of paint. So this is my simple North Country Frame quilt – and I like it very much.

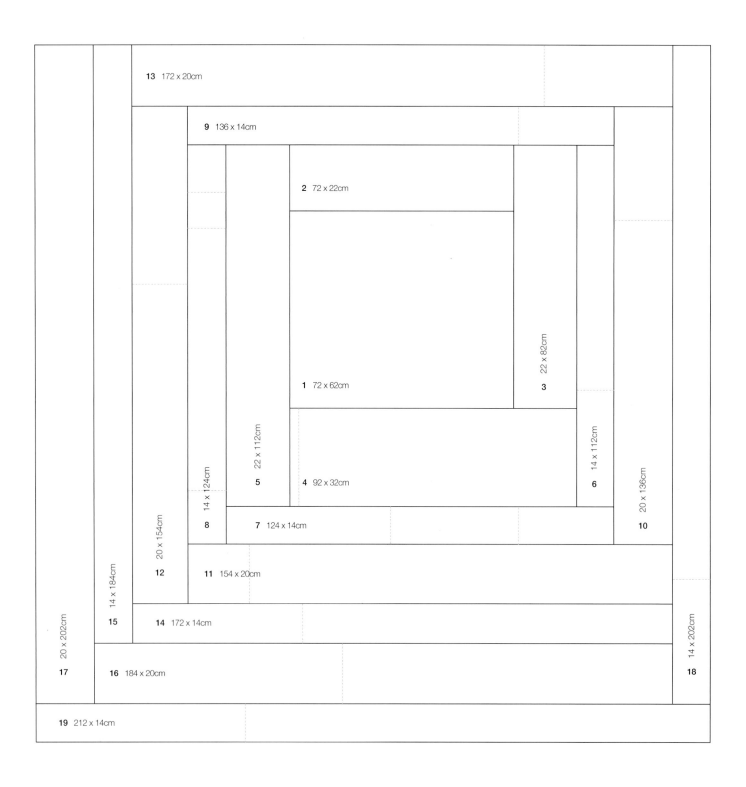

13 172 x 20cm

9 136 x 14cm

2 72 x 22cm

22 x 82cm

1 72 x 62cm

3

22 x 112cm

14 x 112cm

14 x 124cm

5

4 92 x 32cm

6

20 x 154cm

20 x 136cm

8

7 124 x 14cm

10

14 x 184cm

12

11 154 x 20cm

20 x 202cm

15

14 172 x 14cm

14 x 202cm

17

16 184 x 20cm

18

19 212 x 14cm

'After sewing the five central pieces, you can plan the exact placement of the remaining strips or work freestyle.'

QUILT SIZE

212 x 212cm when trimmed and bound. All seam allowances are 1cm and are included in the cutting sizes.

QUILT TOP

You will need approximately 5–6m of fabric. You can use all new fabric or mix in scraps from your stash or other projects. There are five large central pieces, between 72cm and 112cm in length, so make sure you have individual pieces of cloth that are large enough for these. The rest of the quilt is created from long strips, which can be individual pieces or different fabrics joined together for the required length. Look at the diagram and photograph on pages 54–5 to see how it comes together.

I started my quilt with a piece of black and ivory cotton toile. I had just over 1m, so I planned exactly where I wanted it to go in the design. I already had the gorgeous black khadi cotton, linen and ivory canvas, as I was using them throughout the collection of quilts in the book. It was simply a matter of planning, adding and ordering the rest of the fabric to fit what I already had.

QUILT BACKING

You will need approximately 5m of fabric. The finished size should be at least 232 x 232cm, so you can make your backing from fabric leftovers, a sari or a bolt of African wax print, if you like. Piece together your choices until you have the required size.

BINDING

You will need approximately 0.5m of fabric. You can use up any leftovers from the quilt top, or introduce a new fabric for the binding.

I used scraps from the quilt top to tie everything together.

OTHER MATERIALS

WADDING of your choice, 232 x 232cm.
SEWING THREAD 100 per cent cotton all-purpose thread is best, in a neutral colour.
QUILTING THREAD 100 per cent cotton quilting thread in a colour of your choice.

CUT YOUR FABRIC

The simple North Country Frame quilt is a very easy quilt to cut and piece. Similar in ease of construction to the Utility quilt (see page 88), it is also pieced like a very large and simplified Log Cabin block (see page 132).

To make the most of this quilt design, you need to plan your first five pieces (1–5 on the diagram on page 54). Go through your fabric selection and work out which fabrics you want to place where – and make sure that you have enough of them before you start cutting. It can help to lay the fabrics out in the rough shape of the quilt design to get a pleasing combination before you make your final choices.

The remaining pieces (6–19) are long strips made up from a combination of fabrics. You can use single fabrics for each strip or join lengths together to create more of a pattern – it is up to you and the fabric you have chosen.

Start by cutting your first five pieces, following the diagram on page 54. Pencil the number on the back of each piece as you cut it, and set it aside.

You then need to cut your remaining fabric into two widths – 14cm and 20cm. You will need a minimum of 13.5m x 14cm and 10.5m x 20cm in total length. You may need more, depending on the number of seams you make.

You are ready to sew.

SEW YOUR QUILT TOP

Clear a large space close to your cutting and sewing area – a bed or clean floor is ideal. You can then lay your pieces down as you sew them, so that you can see the quilt coming together.

Start by sewing your first five pieces together. Follow the diagram and join each piece in the correct order, starting by sewing 1 to 2, and then joining 3, and so on. Press each seam as you stitch it and trim away any loose threads. Continue until all five pieces are sewn together in the order of the diagram.

Like the Ralli quilt (see page 150), you can preplan the exact placement of the remaining strips or join individual lengths together and just freestyle the strips as you sew.

If you choose the first method, follow the diagram on page 54. You need to create individual lengths to fit each strip. So, for piece 6, you need a finished piece of 14 x 112cm. Join a number of pieces together (between one and as many as you want) until you have 14 x 114cm. Press all the seams, trim away excess threads and then cut the strip down to 14 x 112cm. Sew strip 6 to the central piece, using the diagram as your guide; press the seams and trim away the threads. I find it is useful to mark off the strips on the pattern after I have attached them to the quilt. It is very easy to forget what you have

'The joyous design
of the simple North
Country Frame quilt
is another deeply
moving and inspiring
illustration of beauty
triumphing over
circumstance.'

completed on this design if you have to come back to
it. Continue planning, cutting, piecing and joining the
strips until you have finished the quilt top.

If you choose the second method, you simply need
to join your strips of fabric together until you have the
total required length. You may want to create several
sets of lengths, just for physical ease. Starting with piece
6 and using the diagram as your placement guide, pin
and sew the first 14cm-wide strip to the central piece.
As you aren't matching exact measurements, you need
to pin these strips to avoid stretching the seam, and to be
precise. Trim off the excess, press and remove any stray
threads. Continue pinning and sewing, moving around
the quilt, alternating between the 14cm and 20cm strips
where necessary. Follow the diagram to ensure you are
piecing the strips in the right order. You may need to add
further pieces or join strips together as you go. Once you
have attached strip 19, your quilt top is complete.

SEW YOUR QUILT BACKING

The quilt backing needs to be a minimum of 232 x 232cm.
You may have fabric that is already that size, or a surplus
of cloth from the quilt top. Join your choice of fabric
together until you have a backing the correct size. Press
all the seams and trim away any excess threads.

BUILD YOUR QUILT

Put your quilt sandwich together in your preferred
way (see page 182). After you have marked any
necessary quilting lines, machine- or hand-quilt using
your favourite technique (see page 184). Trim the
backing and wadding so that the edges are even and
your quilt is square. Finally, make and attach the
binding (see page 186).

MAKE IT YOURS

The simple North Country Frame
design allows you to make either a
very minimalist or maximalist quilt.
The narrow strips mean you can join as
many or as few pieces together as you
like. You can make the quilt smaller
by leaving off the last few strips or,
of course, larger by adding more. It is
an excellent quilt for using up lots of
project leftovers and is very easy to
come back to if time is short.

AMISH SAWTOOTH

THE AMISH COMMUNITY is as famous for their quilts as for their collective way of living. Their traditional and modest lifestyle is based on their Christian belief system and focused on the values of simplicity, humility, practicality and hard work. Family is the most important aspect of their community and they have been completely self-reliant for more than 300 years.

The Amish people are an Anabaptist sect that emigrated to Pennsylvania from Germany and Switzerland. They first settled in Lancaster County in around 1727, living as farmers and craftsmen in rural settlements and small townships. Everything they made had to have a functional purpose, as well as being beautifully crafted. Quilt-making started in Amish communities in the mid-1800s, once quilts were deemed to be a practical addition to the household. All quilts were made to be used, but far from being thrown together quickly, Amish quilts have become known for the absolute precision of their stitchwork. They were straightforward and uncluttered in design, combining functionality with exquisite craftsmanship.

The fabric used in early Amish quilts was often hand-woven and dyed. Berries and plant fibres were used to create the deep, saturated colours we associate with Amish clothing and quilts. The first designs were utilitarian Wholecloth quilts, made in solid colours. It wasn't until the 1870s that pieced quilts appeared, but these were still simple shapes and rarely in more than four colours. Quilt colours had to be approved by the community bishop to ensure that they adhered to the structure and rules of the Amish way of life. White, stripes and prints were considered worldly (outside the faith) and deemed unacceptable for use. Quilts, however, were permitted to have a much wider and brighter range of colours than Amish clothing.

Like many other quilting tribes, these women were restricted in numerous aspects of their quilt-making, but still managed to create some of the most recognizable and extraordinary quilts in history. The Amish religion discouraged individual expression, but quilt-making let women demonstrate their creativity without breaking any rules. Each quilt was pieced at home by one artisan but was always communally quilted. The Amish faith encouraged kinship within families and the wider community, so quilting bees became a fundamental part of the women's social life.

Even though the Amish still live separately from society in general, their quilts are justifiably world-famous and many Amish women sell their quilts to outsiders as a source of income. They are expensive, but they are the work of true artisans. The Sawtooth is one of the most recognizable of Amish quilt designs. It is believed to be an evolution of the Welsh and North Country Bars quilts. Can you imagine how these different clans came to meet and share their quilting knowledge?

Finished quilt top measures: 138 x 154cm

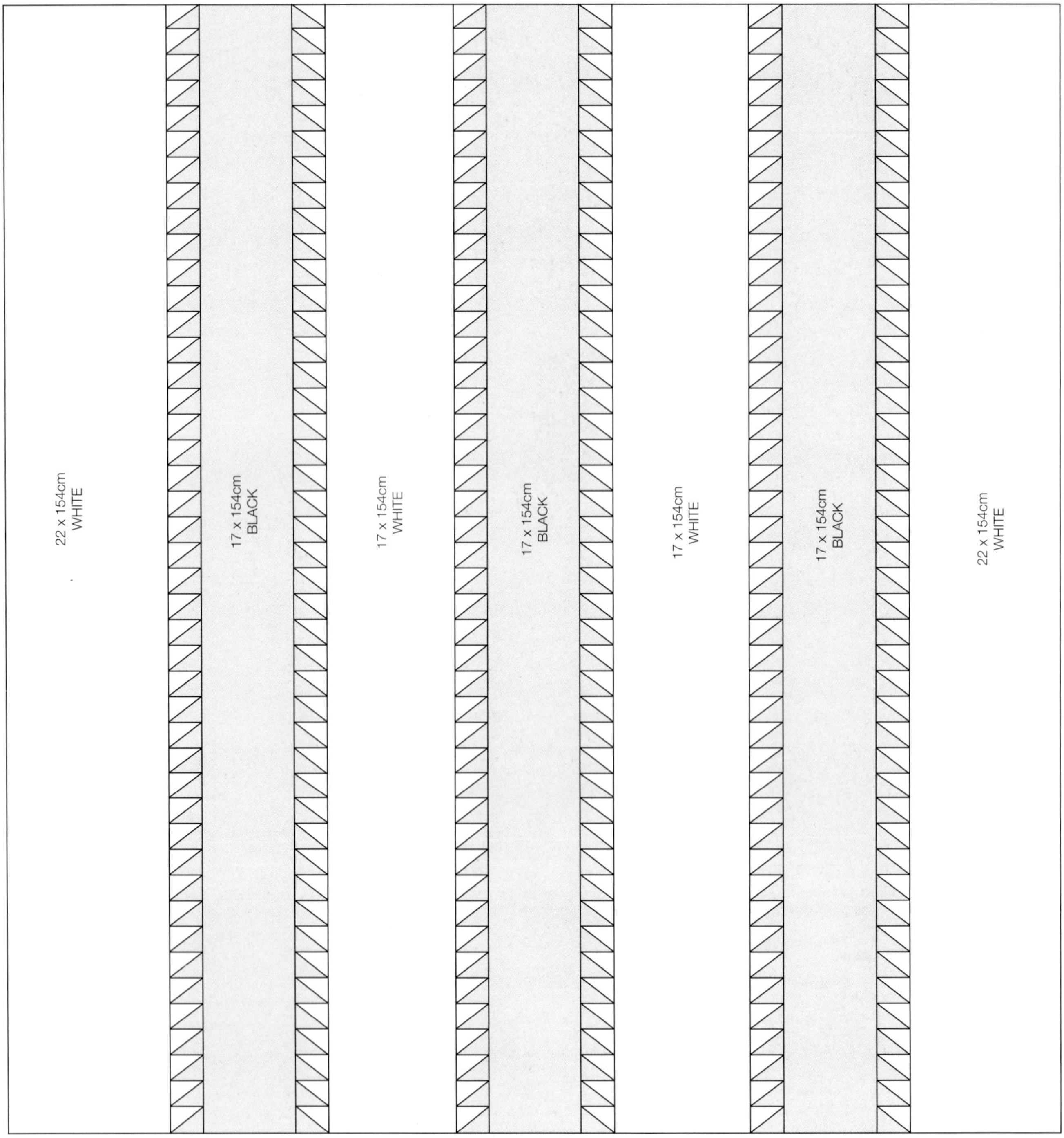
22 x 154cm
WHITE
17 x 154cm
BLACK
17 x 154cm
WHITE
17 x 154cm
BLACK
17 x 154cm
WHITE
17 x 154cm
BLACK
22 x 154cm
WHITE

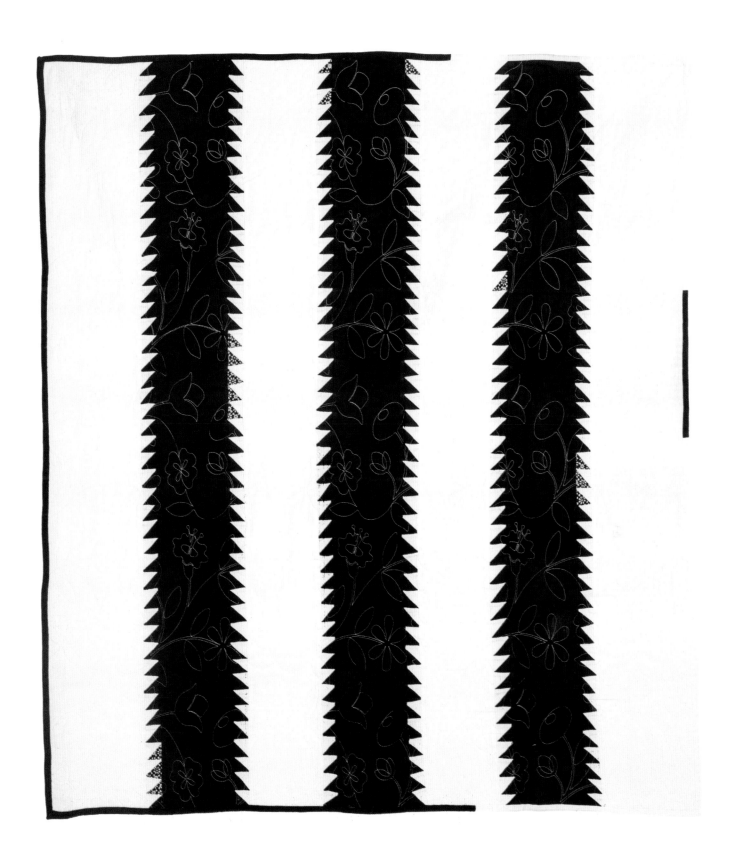

QUILT SIZE
136 x 152cm when trimmed and bound. All seam allowances are 1cm and are already built into the cutting sizes.

QUILT TOP
You will need approximately 3m of fabric A and 2.5m of fabric B. You could also include remnants of a third fabric if you wanted to incorporate patterned 'teeth'.

I used two softly textured khadi cottons – in contrasting ivory and black. I also included a small piece of block-printed Indian cotton to add extra interest – and because I love the print.

QUILT BACKING
You will need approximately 4m of fabric. The finished size should be 156 x 172cm, so you can use left-over cotton or fabric from a bolt of cloth to make the backing.

I had a large piece of ivory khadi to use and paired this with a heavily patterned sari for the backing – a little surprise from the plain and graphic front.

BINDING
You will need approximately 0.5m of fabric. You can use scraps from the quilt top if you have any left over, or use the binding as an opportunity to introduce a new fabric.

I used a mixture of the black and ivory cotton for my binding.

OTHER MATERIALS
WADDING of your choice, 156 x 172cm.
SEWING THREAD 100 per cent cotton all-purpose thread is best, in a neutral colour.
QUILTING THREAD 100 per cent cotton quilting thread in a colour of your choice.

CUT YOUR FABRIC

The cutting is simple but there is a lot of it. This quilt isn't hard to piece, but it can be a little fiddly, so set aside enough time to cut all your fabric in one go and make sure your rotary cutter is very sharp.

In fabric A (ivory), cut the following, cutting the large pieces first:

2 of 22 x 154cm
2 of 17 x 154cm
132 of 6 x 6cm

Cut 6cm-wide strips and then cut them into squares. You can stack three to four layers of fabric on top of each other before you cut, but make sure your blade is sharp and you apply pressure with your quilter's ruler to stop the fabric from sliding. Then cut across each square diagonally to create 264 triangles.

In fabric B (black), cut the following, cutting the large pieces first:

3 of 17 x 154cm
132 of 6 x 6cm

As before, cut 6cm-wide strips, cut them into squares, then cut across each square diagonally to create 264 triangles.

If you want to include any patterned teeth, cut a handful of 6cm squares in your chosen fabric(s) and cut across each square to create diagonals.

You are ready to sew.

SEW YOUR QUILT TOP

Sew one fabric A triangle to one fabric B triangle along the long edge. Be careful not to stretch the seam, as it is cut on the bias. Press the seams towards the darker colour. Repeat for the remaining 263 pairs. To speed up this process, try chain piecing these triangles together (see page 180). Once pressed, trim off the 'ears' and thread.

Divide your squares into two piles. One will be for the upper teeth (with fabric A in the upper left) and one will be for the lower teeth (with fabric A in the upper right). Look at the diagram and photograph on pages 62–3 to see how the teeth run in two directions.

Sew together three upper-teeth rows of 44 squares and three lower-teeth rows of 44 squares. Press all the seams and trim the loose threads.

To piece the quilt top together, look at the diagram on page 62. Sew the first pieces of fabric A (measuring 22 x 154cm) to the first upper-teeth row. Pin securely so that

'This quilt looks best when it is simple and graphic, but it is also the perfect design for including tiny scraps of precious fabric that hold special memories.'

you don't stretch the teeth block. When sewn together, each tooth will measure approximately 3.5 x 3.5cm. Continue pinning and sewing, following the diagram, until you have sewn the last piece of fabric A. Press the seams, snip the threads, and your quilt top is complete.

SEW YOUR QUILT BACKING

Your quilt backing needs to be a minimum of 156 x 172cm. Piece your chosen fabrics together until you have a piece the correct size. Press all the seams, trim away any excess threads, and your quilt backing is complete.

BUILD YOUR QUILT

Put your quilt sandwich together in your preferred way (see page 182). After you have marked any necessary quilting lines, machine- or hand-quilt using your favourite technique (see page 184). Trim the backing and wadding so that the edges are even and your quilt is square. Finally, make and attach the binding (see page 186).

MAKE IT YOURS

This quilt works best with at least one plain fabric, but you could use a small print for the second fabric if you want to include pattern. You can easily increase the size of the quilt by increasing the length, and adding another two or three sections and rows of teeth. If you have very tiny scraps of old baby clothes or a snip from your wedding dress, this is a lovely way to incorporate special memories into a seemingly utilitarian quilt.

HOUSETOP

BECAUSE I RESPECT the quilts and quilters of Gee's Bend so much, I wanted to create another design based on a concept that they embraced. Historically, the Housetop quilt is a utilitarian pattern used by the Amish and Gee's Bend communities, as well as many other cultures around the world. I have seen fantastic British examples – both old and new – and I base many of my quilts on the principles of those designs. At its simplest, it is a very loose form of Log Cabin quilt (see page 132). The key to this is the term 'loose'. Like the Gee's Bend, Utility, Boro and Pojagi quilts (see pages 34, 88, 100 and 138), the Housetop is based on the idea of making the best quilt you can, with the fabric you have, but in a limited time frame.

Although (or perhaps because) the Gee's Bend quilters made the Housetop quilt known, it is a design that has been used extensively when disaster strikes. When people lose their homes or loved ones, quilts are often made as physical protectors and emotional comforters. As the Housetop is easy and quick to piece, and uses fabric at hand, it has become known as an achievable and uplifting solution to a base-level need.

Housetop quilts are incredibly simple to make and that really is the point. You start with one piece of fabric and then build squares or rectangles around it. It is an excellent quilt design for piecing an assortment of fabrics together that are already in your stockpile. Choosing which goes next to what is, I think, the best part of making a quilt – that is, making choices based on your fabric availability and aesthetic, not what someone else tells you to use.

For me, the Housetop really captures what makes quilts so aesthetically, culturally and psychologically compelling. They create something meaningful and necessary out of available materials and then fulfil a real function. They remind us that, at a very basic level, as much as we need a safe roof over our head, it is the necessary objects within that can shape our day-to-day understanding of the world.

My Housetop quilt was a delightful quilt to make and it is very much a favourite in our home. I wanted to stretch the concept of a Log Cabin, so you see that it really is just a matter of cutting and sewing one piece of cloth to another. That is all a quilt is. Plus, I thought it would be great to include a quilt that can be made pretty quickly – the challenging, but fun, part is choosing what combination of fabrics to use and deciding on their layout.

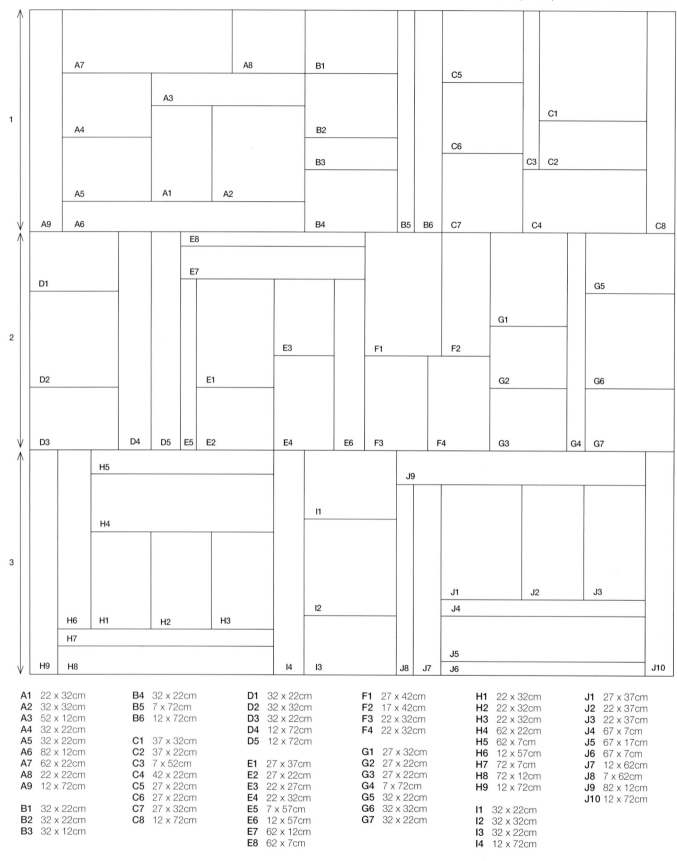

A1 22 x 32cm	**B4** 32 x 22cm	**D1** 32 x 22cm	**F1** 27 x 42cm	**H1** 22 x 32cm	**J1** 27 x 37cm
A2 32 x 32cm	**B5** 7 x 72cm	**D2** 32 x 32cm	**F2** 17 x 42cm	**H2** 22 x 37cm	**J2** 22 x 37cm
A3 52 x 12cm	**B6** 12 x 72cm	**D3** 32 x 22cm	**F3** 22 x 32cm	**H3** 22 x 32cm	**J3** 22 x 37cm
A4 32 x 22cm		**D4** 12 x 72cm	**F4** 22 x 32cm	**H4** 62 x 22cm	**J4** 67 x 7cm
A5 32 x 22cm	**C1** 37 x 32cm	**D5** 12 x 72cm		**H5** 62 x 7cm	**J5** 67 x 17cm
A6 82 x 12cm	**C2** 37 x 22cm		**G1** 27 x 32cm	**H6** 12 x 57cm	**J6** 67 x 7cm
A7 62 x 22cm	**C3** 7 x 52cm	**E1** 27 x 37cm	**G2** 27 x 22cm	**H7** 72 x 7cm	**J7** 12 x 62cm
A8 22 x 22cm	**C4** 42 x 22cm	**E2** 27 x 22cm	**G3** 27 x 22cm	**H8** 72 x 12cm	**J8** 7 x 62cm
A9 12 x 72cm	**C5** 27 x 22cm	**E3** 22 x 27cm	**G4** 7 x 72cm	**H9** 12 x 72cm	**J9** 82 x 12cm
	C6 27 x 22cm	**E4** 22 x 32cm	**G5** 32 x 22cm		**J10** 12 x 72cm
B1 32 x 22cm	**C7** 27 x 32cm	**E5** 7 x 57cm	**G6** 32 x 32cm	**I1** 32 x 22cm	
B2 32 x 22cm	**C8** 12 x 72cm	**E6** 12 x 57cm	**G7** 32 x 22cm	**I2** 32 x 32cm	
B3 32 x 12cm		**E7** 62 x 12cm		**I3** 32 x 22cm	
		E8 62 x 7cm		**I4** 12 x 72cm	

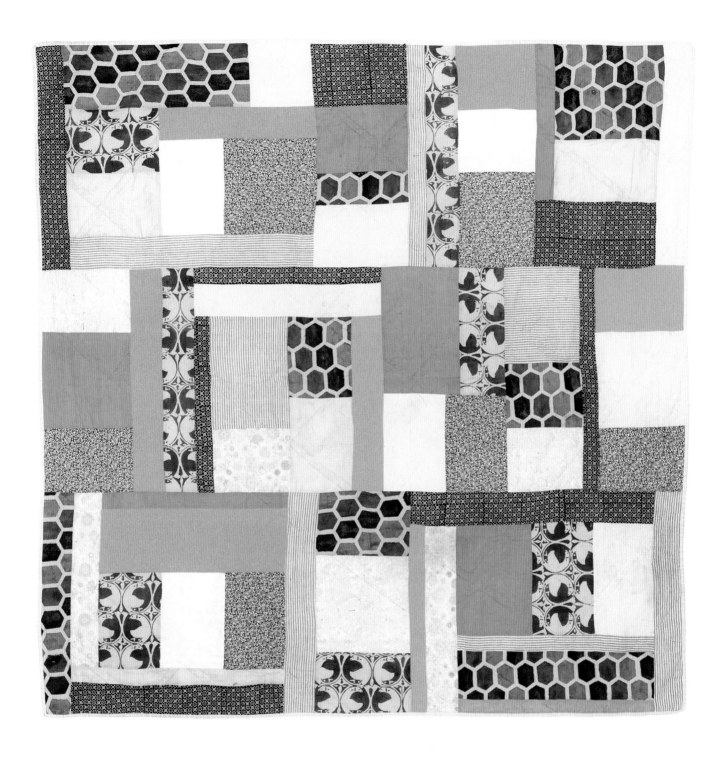

'The Housetop is based on
the idea of making the best
quilt you can with whatever
fabric you have to hand.'

QUILT SIZE

210 x 210cm when trimmed and bound. All seam allowances are 1cm and are included in the cutting sizes.

QUILT TOP

You will need approximately 5.5–6m of fabric. The amount you need depends on the fabric or clothing you are using for your quilt. You might be mixing your husband's old shirts with lovely vintage floral fabrics, or you might be using up some of your fabric stash. The longest piece you need to cut is 82cm, so just make sure you have some fabric this width or length.

I mixed together plain cotton, linen and silk fabrics with a selection of Indian block-prints and Liberty prints. I dyed some of the cotton with herbal teas to achieve the subtle colour palette I wanted.

QUILT BACKING

You will need approximately 5m of fabric. The finished size should be 230 x 230cm, so you can also use fabric leftovers or any other robust cotton, as well as fabric from a bolt of cloth to make the backing.

BINDING

You will need approximately 0.5m of fabric. You can use scraps from the quilt top if you have any left over, or use the binding as an opportunity to introduce a new fabric.

OTHER MATERIALS

WADDING of your choice, 230 x 230cm.
SEWING THREAD 100 per cent cotton all-purpose thread is best, in a neutral colour.
QUILTING THREAD 100 per cent cotton quilting thread in a colour of your choice.

CUT YOUR FABRIC

There are two ways to approach this quilt. Which you choose depends on how confident you are when visualizing fabric combinations. If you are not confident, don't be alarmed, as it is hard to do for a first quilt. As each piece is quite large, take your time rather than cut your fabric incorrectly.

The first way to build the quilt is to create one section at a time – that is, plan, cut and sew section 1, 2 or 3 (see the diagram on page 68) – just concentrating on that section and the blocks within it. Once you have cut and pieced the first section, you can move on to the next one.

The second way is to cut the whole quilt in one go. You will have to make more decisions initially, but you will have slightly more control over the general flow of the quilt. You will also need a space large enough to lay the whole quilt out. With both methods, you will sew the quilt block by block, section by section.

Make sure you have a suitable space to lay everything out, such as a bed, the floor or a wall to pin everything on. From your pile of fabrics, start placing pieces next to each other to get combinations that you like.

For section 1, you have three blocks to cut – A, B and C – but you don't have to start cutting at A1. I often choose and cut the largest pieces first to make sure that I have big enough pieces of fabric available. Don't forget to maximize any small precious cloth, too.

Using the diagram on page 68 as a guide, cut the following pieces:

Section 1: Start with block A. Cut pieces A1–A9, arranging them in the order of the diagram. You can cut them in any order, but it is really important that you lay them out in the correct order. This gives you a chance to change fabrics as you go, rather than ending up with two pieces of the same fabric next to each other. Once you have cut all of block A, pencil the number on the back of each piece and stack them in a pile.

Repeat this process for blocks B and C, and put all three stacks aside.

Section 2: Cut blocks D, E, F and G using the same method as for section 1, cutting and placing the pieces block by block. Put all four stacks aside.

Section 3: Cut blocks H, I and J in the same way and put all three stacks aside.

SEW YOUR QUILT TOP

When you have cut either a section or the whole quilt, you can start to sew it together. Start with section 1, block A. Pull out your pile for block A and just follow the diagram.

First, pin and sew A1 to A2, then press the seam. Then pin and sew A3 to this and press. You have completed a 'block within a block'.

Pin and sew A4 to A5, then press. By looking at the diagram, you can see that you then join the first two blocks together, and then add A6. Next, join A7 to A8, and join them to the larger block. Simply add A9 in the same manner to complete block A.

Once you have got the hang of this method, it is a satisfyingly speedy quilt to sew. After completing block A, move on to blocks B and C.

When you have made up all three blocks in section 1, simply sew them together along the 72cm-long edges. There are a couple of points in the quilt where seamlines match up across the blocks, so make sure you match and pin these accurately before you sew. Press the seams, trim away any threads, and section 1 is complete.

Repeat for sections 2 and 3.

When you have finished all three sections, pin section 1 to section 2, matching up any seamlines as before, and sew them together. Pin section 3 to section 2 in the same manner and then sew together.

Press all the seams and trim away any excess sewing thread. Your quilt top is finished.

SEW YOUR QUILT BACKING

Your quilt backing needs to be a minimum of 230 x 230cm. You may have fabric that is already that size. If not, simply join your choice of fabric together until you have a backing the right size. This can be in strips, squares or freestyle. Press all the seams, trim away any excess threads, and your quilt backing is complete.

BUILD YOUR QUILT

Put your quilt sandwich together in your preferred way (see page 182). After you have marked any necessary quilting lines, machine- or hand-quilt using your favourite technique (see page 184). Trim the backing and wadding so that the edges are even and your quilt is square. Finally, make and attach the binding (see page 186).

MAKE IT YOURS

You can do anything with this quilt. Make only one or two of the sections, or re-order them to suit. This is meant to be a simple quilt that reflects your home and style, so use as few or as many fabrics as you like and make it a size that fits your needs.

WHOLECLOTH

A WHOLECLOTH QUILT was the mark of an artist – the fabric mere canvas on which to express the quilter's fine needlework skills and creative flair. It is a quilt that dates back to the twelfth century, and has been created by European and American artisans alike. A Wholecloth quilt is not necessarily made from a single piece of fabric, but from a few, very large pieces of cloth, and it is then intricately stitched to produce a highly textured, tactile design.

Linen was the most widely used fabric for early European Wholecloth quilts, until cotton was imported from India in the seventeenth century. From 1880, satin cotton in plain colours became the favourite fabric for making these quilts. Its sheen showed the quilting patterns to perfection and encouraged women to improve their stitching prowess. The Arts and Crafts movement inspired women to embrace a simpler decorating style, after the extravagance of the early Victorian era. Plain fabrics were much desired and everyday objects, such as feathers, shells, fans, flowers and leaves, inspired the quilting designs, which were executed in thread in the same colour as the fabric.

Both Welsh and County Durham Wholecloth quilts are highly regarded and extraordinarily beautiful. The design is a signature of both quilting sets and many hundreds travelled with families across the seas. These intricately stitched quilts were prized and carefully stored – they were not your everyday utility quilt, but something that showed the maker's skill, status and creativity. It is often assumed that American quilts began with the early settlers utilizing every scrap of fabric available to make patchwork quilts. However, English and Welsh Wholecloth quilts were some of the first to be found in early colonial homes. Settlers took linen quilts with them, but also created new quilts from a linen and wool mix – linsey-woolsey. This cloth was polished or glazed to make the fabric shine and to prevent the carded wool filling from escaping through the stitching holes.

In the UK, the Rural Industries Board was established after the First World War to encourage the expansion of craft industries in areas suffering economic depression. Women could learn quilt-making through classes, workshops and quilting bees, and go on to make high-quality Wholecloth quilts to sell as luxury items in wealthy areas. The standard of workmanship was raised significantly, as only the very best work was accepted for sale. However, once the Second World War broke out, the production of fabric for quilts seemed to stop overnight. The halcyon period of quilting ceased, as women's lives changed to cope with the extreme demands of war.

My Wholecloth quilt is significantly humbler than the remarkable examples I have seen. The design is based on the two pieces of fabric I chose. There is no grid and no preplanning – just two contrasting yet lovely fabrics stitched together in the style that pleased my eye.

QUILT SIZE

180 x 180cm when trimmed and bound. All seam allowances are 1cm and are already built into the cutting sizes.

QUILT TOP

You will need at least 122 x 182cm of fabric A and 64 x 182cm of fabric B. A Wholecloth quilt needs the fabric to be the hero, so spend time finding two or three pieces of cloth that work beautifully together.

I chose a beautiful block-printed French linen and a Japanese silk for my Wholecloth quilt. I love the tactile combination of linen and silk, and the mixture of faded roses against a plum-coloured shibori print was just fantastic.

Ideally, your central fabric will be cut from one length, so try to find a fabric that is at least 122cm wide.

If your fabric isn't wide enough, you can either add another strip or increase the width of one of the outer strips to compensate.

QUILT BACKING

You will need at least 4m of fabric. The finished size should be 200 x 200cm. Find a contrasting cloth from a bolt or use one of the other quilt designs from this book to create a double-sided quilt. Alternatively, piece some fabric together until you create the right size.

I overdyed a pink fine cotton for my backing – it was a bit too 'pink', so I dyed it in a tea bath to make the colour more subtle and harmonious alongside the two main fabrics.

BINDING

You will need approximately 0.5m of fabric. You can use scraps from the quilt top if you have any left over, or use the binding as an opportunity to introduce a new fabric.

I used left-over strips of the silk to bind my quilt.

OTHER MATERIALS

WADDING of your choice, 200 x 200cm.
SEWING THREAD 100 per cent cotton all-purpose thread is best, in a neutral colour.
QUILTING THREAD 100 per cent cotton quilting thread in a colour of your choice.

CUT YOUR FABRIC

This won't take long.

From fabric A, cut one piece:

122 x 182cm

If you need to join two pieces of fabric together to get the correct width, add another 2cm to your cutting widths to compensate for the extra seam allowance required.

From fabric B, cut two pieces:

42 x 182cm

22 x 182cm

That's it. On to the sewing.

SEW YOUR QUILT TOP

With right sides together, pin and sew your centre strip of fabric A to one of the outer strips of fabric B. Repeat with the second outer strip of fabric B. Press and trim off any threads. Your quilt top is finished.

SEW YOUR QUILT BACKING

Join together your choice of fabric until you have a backing the right size. Press all the seams and trim away any excess threads. Your quilt backing is now complete.

BUILD YOUR QUILT

Put your quilt sandwich together in your preferred way (see page 182). After you have marked any necessary quilting lines, machine- or hand-quilt using your favourite technique (see page 184). Trim the backing and wadding so that the edges are even and your quilt is square. Finally, make and attach the binding (see page 186).

MAKE IT YOURS

This quilt is about both the fabric and the quilting method you choose. I hand-stitched my quilt densely in a free-quilting technique. Depending on your quilting method and how much you quilt them, Wholecloth quilts take on a different look and feel. You can obviously change the size of the quilt and the number of pieces, as well as how many fabrics you use. Maybe just one fabric with long-arm quilting or two pieces with a hand-quilted concentric circle? It is completely your choice.

'This design is based on the two fabrics I chose (and love), as well as the very uplifting concept of free quilting.'

STAR

MANY QUILTING TRIBES have made Star quilts, but this design has taken on a huge cultural significance for Native Americans. In the late nineteenth century the American government moved Indian tribes onto reservations, and this became a difficult period of transition for them. Travelling was restricted, which meant the men weren't allowed to leave the reservations to hunt. They could no longer bring home animal hides for their traditional clothing and bed covers, so the women turned to quilting as an alternative, a skill they were taught by missionaries and at the boarding schools they were required to attend. Eventually they began using the star in their creations, and this particular design developed a spiritual significance.

When we lose control of something, we often hold on tightly to what we have left and project meaning onto it. Whether this is a physical object or a feeling within, it gives us a little power and hope moving forwards. Star quilts became so much more than a functional object to Native Americans. The quilts expressed important cultural and spiritual values of the women who made them. For many, the star was a sacred symbol, connected to personal honour, and many tribes believed in the power of stars overall. The planet Venus was their guiding star, as it represented the direction in which spirits travel from Earth, signifying immortality.

The Morning Star quilt was eventually created and it replaced the role of the traditional red buffalo robe, both physically and spiritually. It was displayed at funerals to honour and protect the loved one on their final journey through the stars, and was also draped around the shoulders of their braves and hunters when they returned from battle or a victorious hunt.

Today, Star quilts are still treasured. They are given to a special friend or family member, newlyweds or new parents. They are gifted to honour a loved one who has died and they are even given to strangers, simply out of respect and admiration. The gift of a handmade quilt was a mark of deference and protection, which I find incredibly moving. Giving something so lovingly created to someone else is a great privilege that we often shy away from.

My Star quilt was created with the notion of giving in mind. I wanted to create a quilt design that could be made easily by one or many, as an effortless gift for someone loved and respected.

Finished quilt top measures: 222 x 222cm

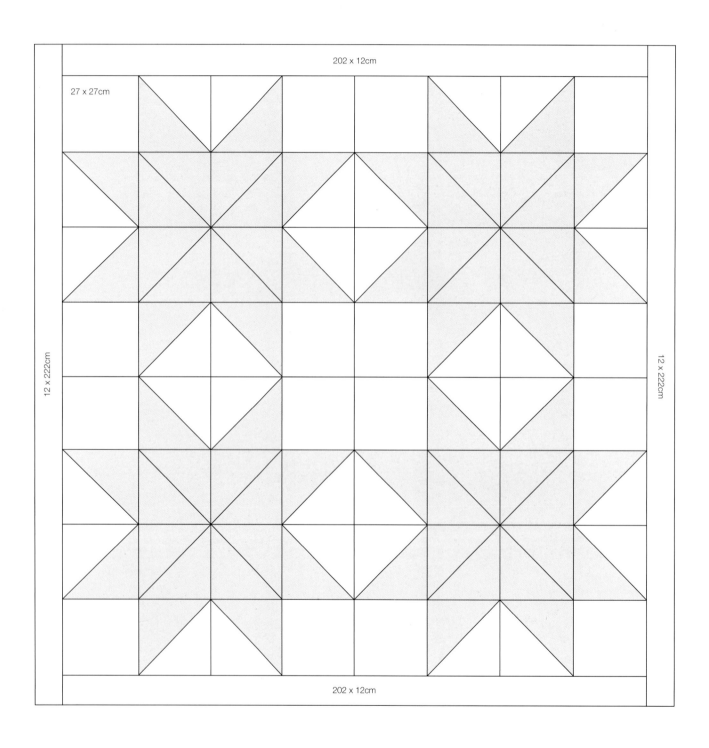

202 x 12cm

27 x 27cm

12 x 222cm

12 x 222cm

202 x 12cm

'The stars can be pieced from a mix
of fabrics or just one, depending on
the effect you wish to create.'

QUILT SIZE
220 x 220cm when trimmed and bound. All seam allowances are 1cm and are already built into the cutting sizes.

QUILT TOP
You will need approximately 3.5m of the outer fabric. This fabric creates the frame around the stars. You will also need approximately 3m of fabric to create the stars. This can be one fabric or a mixture of fabrics, but, ideally, they should have a similar density of colour. Your frame fabric should be in a contrasting colour to your star fabric, in order to create the greatest impact.

For my frame fabric, I used my trusty khadi cotton in cream – it is robust as well as soft, so it works well to contain the stars. I used a wide variety of fabrics for my stars, including Indian silk saris, Japanese cotton, silk velvet and Indian block-printed cottons. Although I used a mix of colours, they all have a similar strength of tone. Some of these fabrics weren't big enough initially, so I quickly pieced several together, which I could then re-cut into the blocks needed. If this all sounds far too complicated and unnecessary, choose just one fabric for the stars.

QUILT BACKING
You will need approximately 5.5m of fabric. The finished size of the backing should be at least 240 x 240cm, so you can make it up from fabric leftovers, a sari or a bolt of African wax print – whatever you fancy. Piece together your choices until you have the size required.

BINDING
You will need approximately 0.5m of fabric. You can use scraps from the quilt top if you have any left over, or use the binding as an opportunity to introduce a new fabric.

I bound my quilt in the cream khadi cotton, so that the frame wasn't interrupted.

OTHER MATERIALS
WADDING of your choice, 240 x 240cm.
SEWING THREAD 100 per cent cotton all-purpose thread is best, in a neutral colour.
QUILTING THREAD 100 per cent cotton quilting thread in a colour of your choice.

'The gift of a quilt was a mark of deference and protection, which I think is incredibly moving.'

CUT YOUR FABRIC
From your outer fabric, cut:
2 of 12 x 202cm
2 of 12 x 222cm
16 of 27 x 27cm
16 of 29 x 29cm
Then cut the 29cm squares diagonally into 32 triangles.
   If you are using one fabric for your stars, cut:
16 of 27 x 27cm
16 of 29 x 29cm
Then cut the 29cm squares diagonally into 32 triangles.
   If you are using multiple fabrics for your stars, cut:
32 of 29 x 29cm
Then cut all of these diagonally into 64 triangles.
   You are ready to sew.

SEW YOUR QUILT TOP
If you are using multiple fabrics for the stars, lay out the triangles in separate piles so that you can see all the different fabrics. Choose two triangles and pin them along the diagonal edge with right sides together. This edge is cut on the bias so will be prone to movement – be vigilant with the pins. Sew the seam together, being careful not to stretch the fabric. Press the seam and trim any excess threads. Repeat 15 times until you have 16 mixed blocks. These will form the centre of the stars.

Use the same method to piece the remaining 32 star triangles to 32 of the outer fabric triangles to form 32 mixed blocks. These will form the outer part of the stars.

Before piecing the quilt top together, trim off any 'tails'. Re-measure and square up your blocks to be accurate.

To piece the quilt top, you have two options. If you are using two fabrics, simply sew the quilt top together in rows by piecing the relevant blocks together. Look at the diagram on page 78 and join a row of 8 blocks together in the correct order. Press the seams and trim loose threads. Repeat this for the remaining seven rows.

Pin the first two rows together, ensuring that you match the seamlines. It is important to be accurate, as the stars need to line up perfectly. Sew, being consistent with your seam allowance. Join all eight rows together in the same way, pressing and trimming threads as you go.

If you have used a variety of fabrics for your stars, it is best to lay the quilt out before you sew it together. Clear a floor or wall space large enough and move the blocks around until you find a composition you are happy with. Photograph it clearly with your phone, camera or tablet, and then sew the quilt top together as above.

To complete the quilt top, pin and sew one 12 x 202cm strip to one edge. Repeat this with the second strip of the same length on the opposite edge. Press the seams. Then pin one 12 x 222cm strip to one of the remaining edges. Repeat with the second strip of the same length on the last edge. Press the seams, remove any loose threads, and your quilt top is complete.

SEW YOUR QUILT BACKING
Your quilt backing needs to be a minimum of 240 x 240cm. You may have fabric that is already that size, or a surplus of cloth from the quilt top. Join your choice of fabric together until you have a backing the correct size. Press all the seams and trim away any excess threads. Your quilt backing is now ready.

BUILD YOUR QUILT
Put your quilt sandwich together in your preferred way (see page 182). After you have marked any necessary quilting lines, machine- or hand-quilt using your favourite technique (see page 184). Trim the backing and wadding so that the edges are even and your quilt is square. Finally, make and attach the binding (see page 186).

MAKE IT YOURS
The Star quilt is marvellous for trying out different techniques. As well as freestyle piecing your fabrics, you could use the String method (see page 106) to create blocks for the stars. You can reverse light and dark, and you can make a small lap quilt or cushion cover by making up one Star block only.

SEMINOLE

THE WORD SEMINOLE means wild – in the context of the Seminole people and their life, it is a perfectly apt description. In 1832 President Jackson ordered that all Native Americans be removed from their land in Florida. The land was rich and fertile, and the new settlers wanted it – so, as settlers around the world often did, they took it. The Seminoles did not give up their land easily, but after several battles, the majority were captured and sent to Oklahoma to live on an Indian reservation. A few hundred managed to escape and sought refuge by disappearing into the Everglades. For several decades they lived quietly, free from the influence of other tribes or intrusion from the outside world.

The first versions of Seminole patchwork evolved out of the fundamental need for clothing. A trip to the closest town took almost a week, so was generally made only once a year. When clothing wore out and cloth ran short, women would make strips out of the remnants from the ends of fabric rolls. These were hand-sewn into larger pieces from which to make clothing and were the beginnings of Seminole piecing. Early designs were simple blocks or bars of alternating colours, or a Sawtooth design (see page 60).

Quilt-making was not originally an important part of the Seminole culture, but it was a natural progression that the distinctive and striking method of strip piecing began to be used for quilts as well as clothing. As is the case for many of the quilting tribes, necessity turned into art.

In around 1900, traders began bringing hand-crank sewing machines and fabric into the Seminole villages. This transformed Seminole patchwork, as the machines made it possible for the women to become more adroit in their sewing and thereby be more creative and elaborate in their designs. They used any fabric that was available, and different clans developed their own patterns as design became increasingly important.

Seminole women have been creating patchwork for nearly a century. Passed down through generations, it is a testament to the adaptability of people under duress, and a reminder that creativity is reliant on only an individual's convictions and ideas.

Piecing Seminole strips feels slightly magical – and it is easy to do. You cut and piece, then re-cut and piece to create incredibly diverse designs. I wanted to showcase Seminole strip piecing, so I created a minimalist backdrop for just a few rows of this wonderful craft. It is an excellent design to use if you have a small remnant of something beautiful, or left-over scraps that you want to use up. Seminole piecing offers endless design opportunities, so feel free to adjust or change the designs to suit your own artistic ideals.

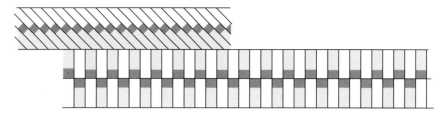

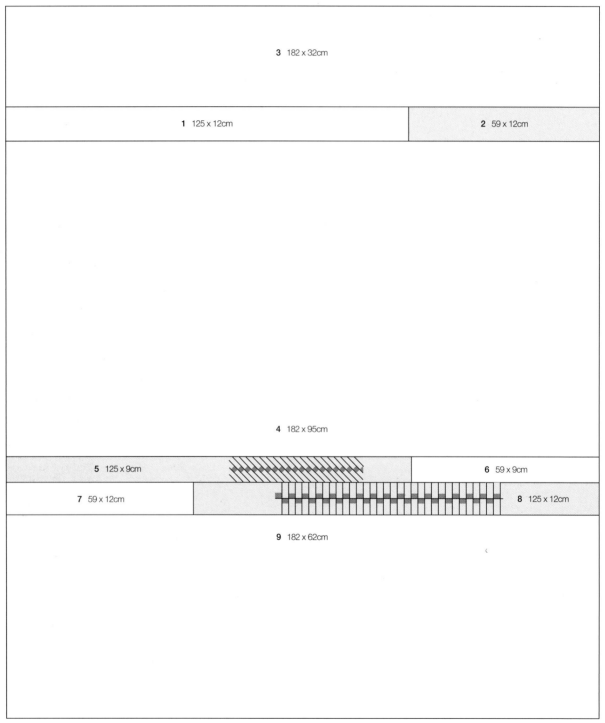

QUILT SIZE

180 x 210cm when trimmed and bound. All seam allowances are 1cm and are included in the cutting sizes.

QUILT TOP

You will need approximately 3.75m of your main fabric.

For Seminole strip 1, you will need 25cm of fabric A, 15cm of fabric B and 20cm of fabric C.

For Seminole strip 2, you will need 20cm of fabric D, 10cm of fabric E and 15cm of fabric F.

I have always wanted to make a predominantly black quilt and I thought that the Seminole design was perfect for this, so I chose some black khadi cotton. The Seminole strips are made from precious remnants of sari silk, Indian block-printed cotton and a lovely soft taupe linen. It is simple but striking.

QUILT BACKING

You will need approximately 5m of fabric. The finished size should be at least 200 x 230cm, so you can use fabric leftovers or fabric from a bolt of cloth to make the backing.

I wanted to contrast the utilitarian nature of the black khadi with something a little more luxurious, as well as complementing the Seminole strips. I chose two contrasting silk saris, which picked out the gold and pale blue of the front detail. I often use saris to back my quilts. The quality, patterns and colours are wonderful, and silk keeps you warm. One sari easily makes at least one backing for a full-size quilt and is a great deal cheaper than simple quilting cotton. Last but not least, most of them are old so are a sustainable resource.

BINDING

You will need approximately 0.5m of fabric. You can use scraps from the quilt top if you have any left over, or use the binding as an opportunity to introduce a new fabric.

I used the excess black khadi to bind this quilt, as I wanted all the focus to be on the Seminole strips.

OTHER MATERIALS

WADDING of your choice, 200 x 230cm.
SEWING THREAD 100 per cent cotton all-purpose thread is best, in a neutral colour.
QUILTING THREAD 100 per cent cotton quilting thread in a colour of your choice.

CUT YOUR FABRIC

Cut your main fabric first. Look at the diagram on page 84, then cut the following and set the pieces aside:

1 of 182 x 95cm
1 of 182 x 62cm
1 of 182 x 32cm
1 of 125 x 12cm
1 of 59 x 12cm
1 of 59 x 9cm

Then cut your chosen fabric for the Seminole piecing into the following lengths:

Fabric A: 8 x 300cm
Fabric B: 4 x 300cm
Fabric C: 6 x 300cm
Fabric D: 8 x 170cm
Fabric E: 4 x 170cm
Fabric F: 7 x 170cm

You are ready to sew.

SEW YOUR QUILT TOP

First, you need to sew, cut and re-sew the Seminole strips together. Although this technique is a little time-consuming, it is super-simple and incredibly effective.

Reduce the stitch length on your sewing machine. Pin and sew fabric A to fabric B along one long edge, being careful not to stretch the fabric. Pin and sew fabric C to the other long edge of fabric B, changing the direction of sewing as you do this to prevent the seam from curving. (Look at the Ralli quilt, on page 150, for more information on why this is important.) Press the seams open and trim away excess thread.

Cut the strip into 5cm sections. Turn every other section by 180° so that alternate designs are reversed, and stitch them back together in a long strip – look at the diagram and photograph on pages 84–5. Press the seams and trim the excess threads. Cut the strip into two pieces measuring 125 x 12cm and 59 x 12cm.

Pin and sew fabric D to fabric E along one long edge, being careful not to stretch the fabric. Pin and sew fabric F to the other long edge of fabric E, changing the direction of sewing to prevent the seam from curving. Press the seams open and trim away excess thread.

Cut the strip into 5cm sections. Reposition the pieces diagonally, so that the right corner of fabric E on the first piece matches the left corner of fabric E on the second piece – again, look at the diagram and photograph on

'Seminole piecing feels slightly magical. You cut and piece, then re-cut and piece to create incredibly diverse designs.'

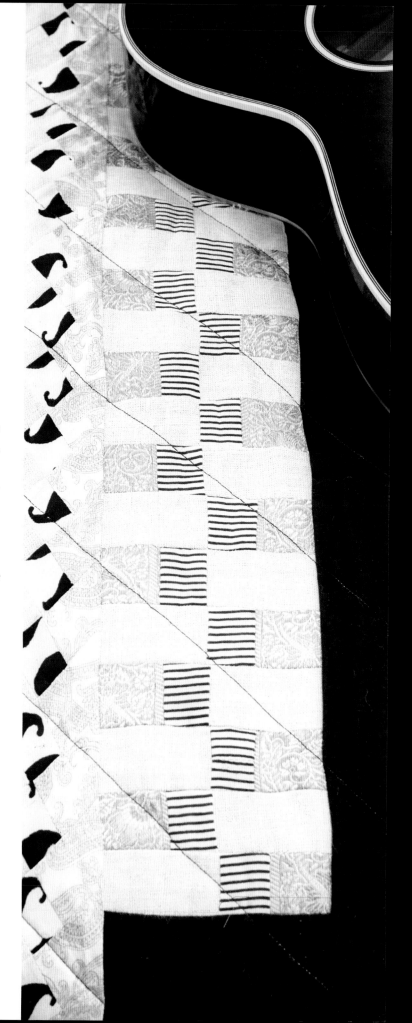

pages 84 5. Stitch the pieces together, press the seams and cut the threads. Trim off the points along both long sides, leaving the seam allowance. Trim the strip to 125 x 9cm.

Follow the diagram to piece the quilt top together, joining the blocks in the correct order according to their piece number (that is, join 1 to 2, then join that to 3 before adding 4, and so on). Pin all the pieces to avoid stretching, especially Seminole strip 2, which is cut on the bias. Press the seams, trim any threads and your quilt top is complete.

SEW YOUR QUILT BACKING

Your quilt backing needs to be a minimum of 200 x 230cm. Join your choice of fabric together until you have a backing the right size. Press all the seams and trim away any excess threads. Your quilt backing is now complete.

BUILD YOUR QUILT

Put your quilt sandwich together in your preferred way (see page 182). After you have marked any necessary quilting lines, machine- or hand-quilt using your favourite technique (see page 184). Trim the backing and wadding so that the edges are even and your quilt is square. Finally, make and attach the binding (see page 186).

MAKE IT YOURS

If you have the patience, the Seminole technique can be used to create a complete quilt. You can vary the width of the strips and how many pieces of fabric you use in a strip – it is a great opportunity for experimenting. You can also change the width of the quilt or adjust the length and composition of the Seminole strips within it.

UTILITY

THERE IS A DICTIONARY definition of a Utility quilt stating that it is 'A plain, basic quilt meant to be used for everyday bedding.' Although I believe that all quilts should be used every day, a Utility quilt was seen as something to rustle up quickly – the artistic skill of its maker wasn't important, but its function was. I have seen Utility quilts that are breathtakingly beautiful, not only for their naïve design and structure, but also because of their purpose. Unfortunately, very few Utility quilts have lasted well. I hope this is because they were used and loved until they had done their job.

The Utility quilt has its roots in recycling. Hoarded scraps, worn clothing and traveller's sample books (from which housewives could order fabrics) were combined to create practical, workaday quilts. It was a way of extending the use of a resource that was in short supply; fabric could never be thrown away – there was always something useful to be made from it.

Utility quilts were definitely made in Europe alongside other quilt styles, but the quilts made by the early American settlers were all strictly utilitarian. They were born of necessity rather than design, as the women needed to provide warm covers for beds, doors and draughty windows. The earliest settlers' quilts were used to sleep under and sit on, and to block light, rain and wind, and were so intimately connected to the very basic functions of living that very little thought was given to them beyond their primary function. During the early years of colonization, women were so busy sewing clothes for their family that they had little time for artistic pursuits. Fabric sources were scarce and often controlled, so women had to be creative with the fabric they had to hand. If a quilt wore through, it was patched or used as wadding for a new quilt. This recycling was done quickly to ensure the family stayed warm in harsh conditions.

There is something universally appealing about a Utility quilt. The need to reuse textiles is global and timeless. I believe that the fundamental necessity of these quilts brought about remarkable innovation. Perhaps because the woman were restricted by time, money and resources, their creativity was, in fact, less restricted. There was no time to ponder perfect corners or stitch lengths while creating a simple, functional piece of family history. What could be more innovative than that?

Although my Utility quilt does have a pattern to follow, I hope that it still feels free, simple and useful. It came together very quickly and was incredibly satisfying to piece. It is guaranteed to be on a bed/sofa/child/dog in someone's home very soon.

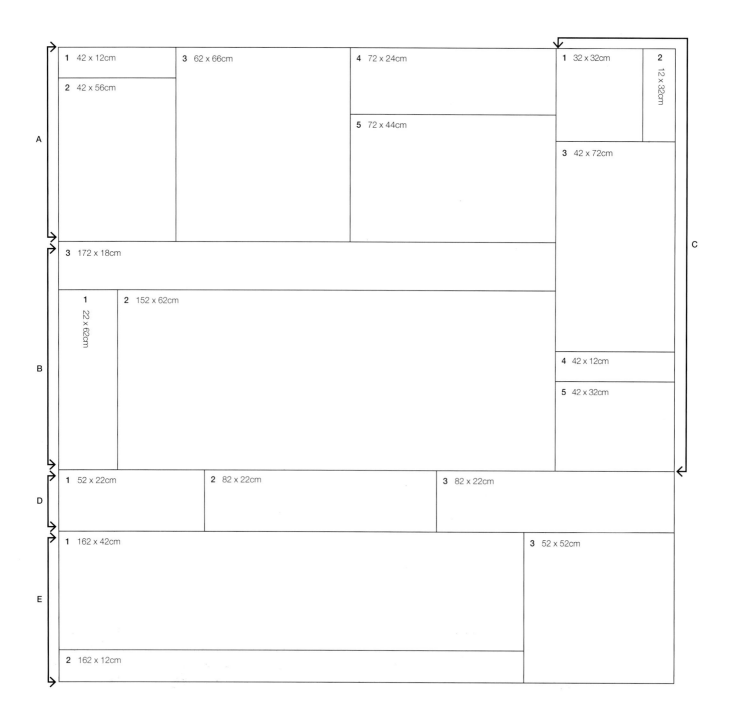

A

1 42 x 12cm
2 42 x 56cm
3 62 x 66cm
4 72 x 24cm
5 72 x 44cm
1 32 x 32cm
2 12 x 32cm
3 42 x 72cm

B

3 172 x 18cm
1 22 x 62cm
2 152 x 62cm
4 42 x 12cm
5 42 x 32cm

C

D

1 52 x 22cm
2 82 x 22cm
3 82 x 22cm

E

1 162 x 42cm
3 52 x 52cm
2 162 x 12cm

'Simple blocks of humble fabrics can make a quilt of great beauty.'

QUILT SIZE

210 x 210cm when trimmed and bound. All seam allowances are 1cm and are already built into the cutting sizes.

QUILT TOP

You will need approximately 5–6m of fabric. The most important thing is to ensure that you have a large enough piece of cloth for the central piece, which measures 152 x 62cm. I advise that you look at the diagram on page 90 and preplan each fabric choice, so that you know exactly how much you need of each cloth to create the look and feel you want.

I started my quilt with a heavily embroidered vintage silk sari, which made a wonderful centre point. Its base colour is cherry-red, but the print also features pink, ivory, yellow and black, so these hues became my palette. I already had the gorgeous black khadi cotton, the linen and the ivory canvas, as I was using these throughout the collection of quilts in the book. So it was simply a matter of planning, adding and ordering the rest of the fabric to fit what I already had.

QUILT BACKING

You will need approximately 5m of fabric. The finished size should be at least 230 x 230cm, so you can use fabric leftovers or new fabric from a bolt of cloth to make the backing.

BINDING

You will need approximately 0.5m of fabric. You can use scraps from the quilt top if you have any left over, or use the binding as an opportunity to introduce a new fabric.

I used scraps from the quilt top, as I didn't want to distract from the very simple, yet bold, quilt design.

OTHER MATERIALS

WADDING of your choice, 230 x 230cm.
SEWING THREAD 100 per cent cotton all-purpose thread is best, in a neutral colour.
QUILTING THREAD 100 per cent cotton quilting thread in a colour of your choice.

CUT YOUR FABRIC

Once you have planned your design, this is an extremely simple quilt to cut and piece – utility in both design and construction. Using the diagram on page 90 as a guide, cut out each piece of fabric as planned. You don't have to cut them in order, but do mark the number of the piece on the back with a pencil or tailor's chalk. I would cut all the pieces you want from one particular fabric, set those aside and then move on to the next fabric.

These are large pieces to cut, so make sure you give yourself plenty of room to slide the fabric across, up and down your cutting mat. Once you have cut all the pieces, you are ready to sew your quilt together.

SEW YOUR QUILT TOP

The Utility quilt design is made up of five (large) blocks. Starting with block A, sew A1 to A2. Press the seam and trim any loose threads. Then sew A3 to this block, press and trim the threads. Sew A4 to A5, press and trim loose threads. Then sew this to block A1/A2/A3. Press the seam, trim the threads and your first block is complete. Continue this method until you have completed all five blocks.

To complete the quilt top, sew all five blocks together in the following order (referring to the diagram), pressing the seams and trimming the threads as you go:

Block A to Block B
Block C to Block A/B
Block D to Block A/B/C
Block E to Block A/B/C/D
Press the seams again, and your quilt top is finished.

SEW YOUR QUILT BACKING

Your quilt backing needs to be a minimum of 230 x 230cm. Join your choice of fabric together until you have a backing the right size. Press all the seams, trim away any excess threads, and your quilt backing is complete.

BUILD YOUR QUILT

Put your quilt sandwich together in your preferred way (see page 182). Machine- or hand-quilt using your favourite technique (see page 183). Trim the backing and wadding so that the edges are even and your quilt is square. Finally, make and attach the binding (see page 186).

MAKE IT YOURS

The beauty of a Utility quilt lies in its simplicity. It is meant to be pieced quickly from what you have, so raid your fabric stash and look in cupboards and wardrobes to see what you can reuse.

CANADIAN RED CROSS

TO MAKE A QUILT and give it to someone you know and love is a wonderful thing – it takes time and commitment on many levels – but to make thousands of quilts to send to people you will never know is quite another. The devastation created by the Second World War for many British people is well documented. They lost their possessions, their homes and, of course, their loved ones. Many organizations rallied together to provide food, blankets and a temporary roof over people's heads. Crucial to this support were the sewing rooms of the Canadian Red Cross.

Hundreds of thousands of quilts were made by Canadian women and sent to Britain throughout the war. The quilts were given to the newly homeless, to hospitals, crèches and refuges, as well as to those in the armed forces. The Red Cross gathered these women together to piece as many quilts as they could. The quilts were simple and utilitarian in design, created from any fabrics that they could get their hands on. Everything from worn-out clothes and scraps of furnishing fabrics to flannelette sheets were used to maximize the number of quilts they could make. Even Victorian Crazy quilts made a comeback, once the women needed to dig deeper into their scrap bags. No predetermined patterns or designs were set – it was completely up to the individual to choose the style and complexity of their quilts, with an emphasis on speed and prolificness. The quilts were made quickly, machine-pieced and hand-quilted, but although the simple stitched patterns reflected wartime pragmatism, they also expressed the makers' creativity.

We often like to share our story if we have done something lovely for somebody else. There isn't anything wrong with that – it is a just reward for giving. Amazingly, we will never know who made these quilts, as the makers had to remain anonymous. The only identification was a small label printed with 'Gift of the Canadian Red Cross'. But we know there are stories of women walking through mud and sleet to get to the sewing centres, including a widowed mother of 18 children who walked 18 miles every week to make quilts throughout the war. We also know that thousands of women made these quilts and that they arrived in tens of thousands – in just one six-week period in 1944, Britain received 25,000 Canadian quilts. Hardly any of these quilts remain in the public eye today; perhaps they were used until they were threadbare, or perhaps they are stored and treasured for the comfort they provided. Wherever they are, these quilts should remind us that giving is good, and to give is often all the reward we need.

My interpretation of a Red Cross quilt uses scraps from many of the other quilts in the book, as it just seemed right to make something beautiful out of very little. With its simple cross design, it is a quick but heartening quilt to make.

Finished quilt top measures: 182 x 182cm

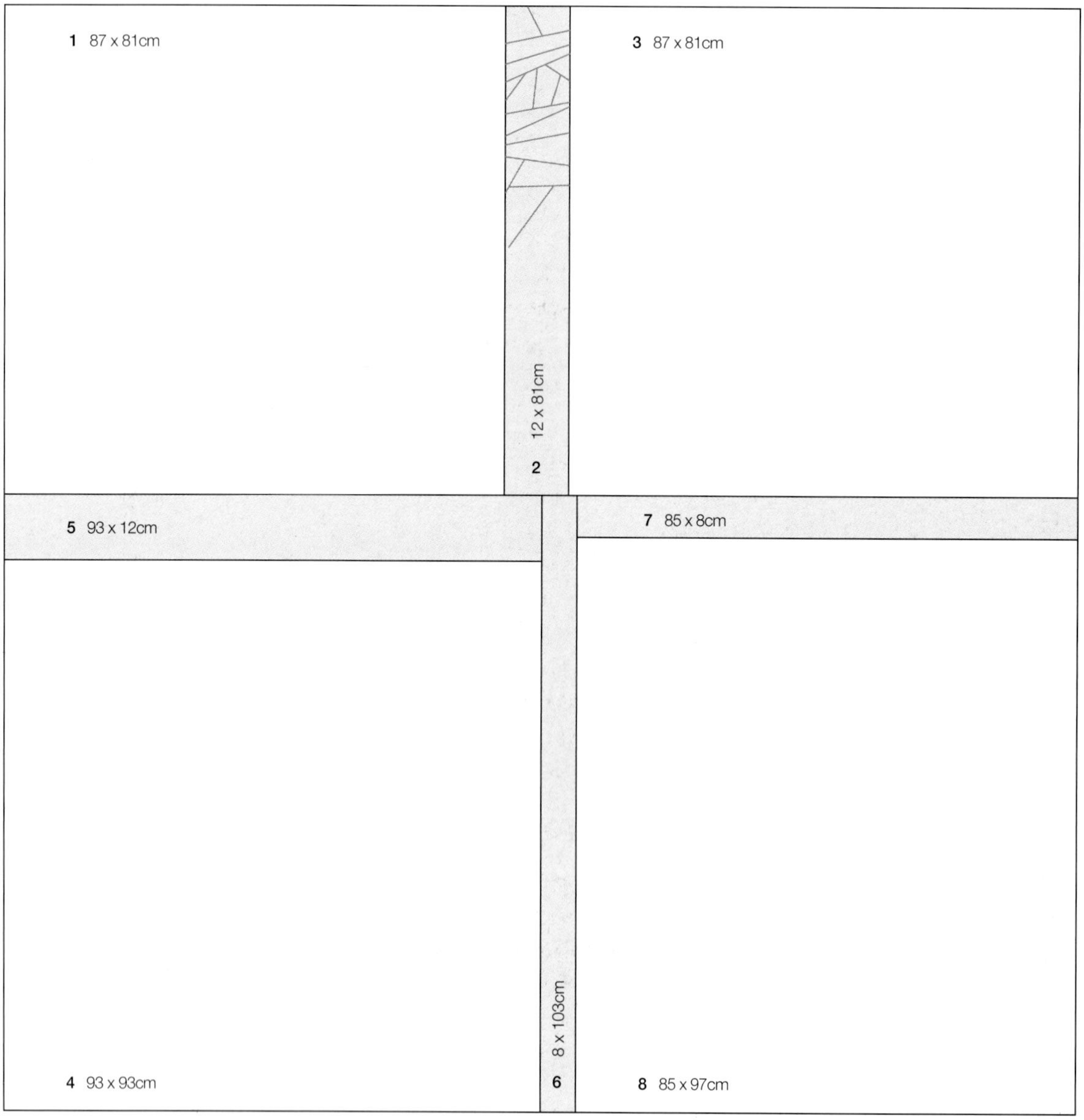

1 87 x 81cm
12 x 81cm
2
3 87 x 81cm
5 93 x 12cm
7 85 x 8cm
8 x 103cm
4 93 x 93cm
6
8 85 x 97cm

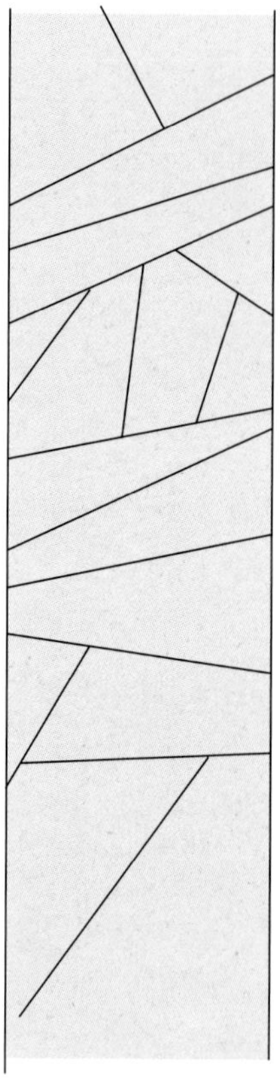

'Use any scraps that you have for the "crazy" cross and enjoy making something beautiful out of very little.'

QUILT SIZE

180 x 180cm when trimmed and bound. All seam allowances are 1cm and are already built into the cutting sizes.

QUILT TOP

You will need approximately 3.75m of background fabric. This fabric surrounds your 'crazy' cross. Due to standard fabric widths, you will have some wastage, but you can always use that on the quilt back. This design works best if you use the same fabric for all four sections so the cross stands out, but it can, of course, be any colour or pattern. You will also need a small pile of scraps to create the central cross. Each piece can be any size, so almost all remnants can be used.

I used a fine ivory organic cotton for my background fabric, as it had a lovely handle and sheen. I then gathered cloth remnants from any of the quilts where I had already used blue, grey, green or natural linen fabrics. At the last minute, I snaffled a tiny scrap of the red sari fabric that I had used in the wonderful Utility quilt (see page 88) – this is a Red Cross quilt, after all.

QUILT BACKING

You will need approximately 4m of fabric. The finished size should be at least 200 x 200cm, so you can use fabric leftovers, a sheet or any other robust cotton, as well as fabric from a bolt of cloth to make the backing.

I used a large swathe of the red sari silk to create a dynamic contrast.

BINDING

You will need approximately 0.5m of fabric. You can use scraps from the quilt top if you have any left over, or use the binding as an opportunity to introduce a new fabric.

I used the ivory cotton left over from the quilt top so that the binding disappeared within the overall design.

OTHER MATERIALS

WADDING of your choice, 200 x 200cm.
SEWING THREAD 100 per cent cotton all-purpose thread is best, in a neutral colour.
QUILTING THREAD 100 per cent cotton quilting thread in a colour of your choice.

CUT YOUR FABRIC

Referring to the diagram on page 96, begin by cutting out the four background pieces of cloth. Mark the corresponding number of the piece on the back with a pencil or tailor's chalk. The rest of your quilt is cut and pieced together at the same time, so you are ready to sew.

SEW YOUR QUILT TOP

Press your scrap cloth so that you have flat pieces of fabric to work with. Spread your fabrics out near your cutting mat so that you can draw easily from each pile. The cross is pieced in a modern version of crazy quilting. Traditional crazy quilts require you to sew each piece to a backing fabric or paper, but you can achieve the same effect simply by cutting and stitching pieces with right sides together. It is a similar technique to the Gee's Bend and String quilts (see pages 34 and 106), as there is no preplanning, but the pieces are smaller and randomly shaped.

Choose your first piece of fabric and cut it to any size and shape you like. Choose a second piece of fabric and cut it, making sure that one edge of each piece is the same length or slightly longer. Sew these first two pieces together along that edge (you can use a narrower seam allowance for this technique), finger-press the seam flat, trim if need be, and cut any threads. Cut a third piece of fabric, making sure one edge is longer than the edge you want to join it to. Sew, finger-press and trim the excess.

Continue cutting, sewing, turning and trimming, building up a largish piece of crazy quilting. This will be a randomly shaped, wiggly-edged piece of cloth of any size. You don't need to build the cross into its exact proportions (that would be ridiculously hard work). Just cut the widths you need from the large piece and use the off-cuts to start the next piece. Look at the diagram and photograph on pages 96–7 to see how these pieces come together.

Use your rotary cutter to trim one edge straight. Then cut a 12cm strip. Continue to cut 12cm strips until you have roughly the length of block 2 (allowing for seam allowances when you join them together). Trim the short ends of each strip so that they are square and can be joined in a straight line – this is important. Sew your pieces together, press, then trim block 2 to 12 x 81cm. Join the leftovers together, and continue to cut, sew and piece until you have made the three remaining 'crazy' blocks.

Join the quilt together in the order of the diagram:
Join block 1 to block 2, then block 3 to block 2.
Join block 4 to block 5, then block 6 to block 4/5.
Join block 7 to block 8. Join block 7/8 to block 4/5/6.
Join this block to block 1/2/3.

Press all the seams, trim away any excess sewing thread, and your quilt top is finished.

SEW YOUR QUILT BACKING

The quilt backing needs to be a minimum of 200 x 200cm. Join your choice of fabric together until you have a backing the right size. It can be strips, squares or freestyle, or one large piece of fabric. Press the seams, trim any threads, and your quilt backing is complete.

BUILD YOUR QUILT

Put your quilt sandwich together in your preferred way (see page 182). After you have marked any necessary quilting lines, machine- or hand-quilt using your favourite technique (see page 184). Trim the backing and wadding so that the edges are even and your quilt is square. Finally, make and attach the binding (see page 186).

MAKE IT YOURS

The Canadian Red Cross quilt can take on a variety of personalities, depending on your choice of fabrics. A patterned background fabric would change its look and feel, as would a reverse composition of light and dark fabrics. The 'crazy' cross would be a wonderful opportunity to use fragments of antique silks and velvets or meaningful remnants; any tattered edges can be trimmed away and special fabrics can be easily distributed. The size of the quilt can also be reduced or increased with a few simple calculations. The spirit of this quilt obviously means it is a perfect quilt to make and then give to someone else – stay anonymous if you can.

BORO

FROM ITS DEFINITION – broken or worn to tatters, then extensively repaired to survive beyond its expected life cycle – it doesn't seem that Boro should be beautiful, but it truly is, both aesthetically and spiritually.

Boro was born from the idea of *mottainai*, a Japanese term that meant 'too good to waste'. Cotton and hemp scraps were lovingly patched and repaired to create bedding and clothing that would last a lifetime and beyond. The magic of Boro is not just the indigo palette we all love, or even the on-trend 'up-cycling' aspect of it. Boro, most importantly, is about family; it is about birth, death and everything in between, all recorded by patches of fabric and thread. Sewn together over generations, its seams are woven through with a family's story and history. Boro reminds us to appreciate the value of time rather than money and shows us that beauty really isn't about acquisition.

Peasants, merchants and artisans in Japan wore Boro clothing from the Edo period (1615–1868) to the early Showa period (1926–89). Silk kimonos and intricate obis were available to only the aristocratic few, but Boro was deemed beautiful because of its craftsmanship. The sewing and weaving skills were highly sophisticated and individual creativity was valued. Once clothing was made, it would be maintained throughout the owner's lifetime and longer. For peasant families, every garment or piece of bedding would last long enough to be passed down through generations. Futons and sheets were also created with the Boro technique, and whole families slept together on and under them. The extraordinary *bodoko*, or 'life-cloth', was a bed sheet for day-to-day use, but it was also used as a birthing sheet. It is quite magical to think that the first thing a brand new baby touched were the clothes of its ancestors.

Like early North American patchwork quilts, Boro cloth reveals so much about the Japanese standard of living and the economy of their time. Women would continually repair clothes and bedding by patching fabric scraps over thin areas and holes in the fabric, to ensure longevity. After the Second World War, the Japanese people regarded Boro textiles with great shame. The utilitarian nature of the cloth was a reminder of an impoverished past, yet these same textiles are now loved and collected for the stories they tell about Japanese folk culture and the long thread of family history.

My quilt is a mere homage to true Boro, but I hope that you can take inspiration from the genesis of Boro within your own quilt. Include cloth, time and stories from your family – old and new – and create a Boro quilt that will last a lifetime or three.

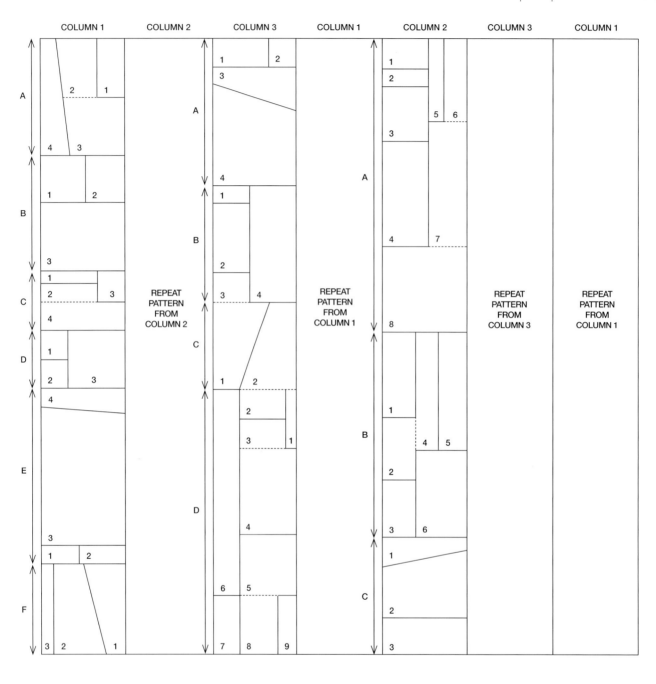

COLUMN 1					
A1	12 x 22cm	**D1**	12 x 12cm		
A2	16–14 x 22cm	**D2**	12 x 12cm		
A3	24–22 x 22cm	**D3**	22 x 22cm		
A4	8–12 x 42cm				
		E1	16 x 8cm		
B1	18 x 18cm	**E2**	18 x 8cm		
B2	16 x 18cm	**E3**	32 x 50–48cm		
B3	32 x 26cm	**E4**	32 x 8–10cm		
C1	22 x 6cm	**F1**	16–8 x 32cm		
C2	22 x 8cm	**F2**	14–22 x 32cm		
C3	12 x 12cm	**F3**	6 x 32cm		
C4	32 x 12cm				

COLUMN 3

A1	22 x 12cm	**D1**	6 x 22cm		
A2	12 x 12cm	**D2**	18 x 12cm		
A3	32 x 8–16cm	**D3**	18 x 12cm		
A4	32 x 36–28cm	**D4**	22 x 32cm		
		D5	22 x 22cm		
B1	16 x 8cm	**D6**	12 x 72cm		
B2	16 x 26cm	**D7**	12 x 22cm		
B3	16 x 12cm	**D8**	16 x 22cm		
B4	18 x 42cm	**D9**	8 x 22cm		
C1	22–12 x 32cm				
C2	12–22 x 32cm				

COLUMN 2

A1	18 x 12cm	**B1**	14 x 31cm
A2	18 x 8cm	**B2**	14 x 23cm
A3	18 x 20cm	**B3**	14 x 22cm
A4	18 x 36cm	**B4**	10 x 42cm
A5	8 x 30cm	**B5**	12 x 42cm
A6	10 x 30cm	**B6**	20 x 32cm
A7	16 x 44cm		
A8	32 x 32cm	**C1**	32 x 12–6cm
		C2	32 x 20–26cm
		C3	32 x 14cm

'Boro is about family; it is about
birth, death and everything
in between, all recorded by
patches of fabric and thread.'

QUILT SIZE
210 x 210cm when trimmed and bound. All seam allowances are 1cm and are included in the cutting sizes.

QUILT TOP
You will need approximately 5–6m of fabric. This can be a mixture of fabric cut from bolts and scraps (or clothing) – you need to be able to cut pieces from 12 x 12cm up to 72cm long.

I used eight or nine different fabrics and included plains, stripes and small prints, all within an indigo colour scheme. I mixed together Indian block-printed cotton, plain shirting, hand-woven khadi cotton and a few precious pieces of Japanese cloth, all of similar weights. I made sure I included enough ivory cotton to provide 'light relief' to the variety of blues. Make sure you wash any cloth that has been hand-woven or dyed, as natural dyes do 'leak'. See page 169 for more on fabric.

QUILT BACKING
You will need approximately 5m of fabric. The finished size should be at least 230 x 230cm. You can use leftovers from your quilt top, a sheet or sari, or fabric from a bolt of cloth.

I hotfooted it down to my local African fabric store for a bolt of indigo and white wax-print cotton – just perfect for this quilt. I gave it a quick wash to remove size and excess dye, then cut the bolt in half and stitched it back together along the long edge to make the backing.

BINDING
You will need approximately 0.5m of fabric. You can use fabric scraps from the quilt top if you have any left over, or use the binding as an opportunity to introduce a new fabric.

I used ivory cotton from the quilt top to keep it light.

OTHER MATERIALS
WADDING of your choice, 230 x 230cm.
SEWING THREAD 100 per cent cotton all-purpose thread is best, in a neutral colour.
QUILTING THREAD 100 per cent cotton quilting thread in a colour of your choice.

CUT YOUR FABRIC

The Boro quilt looks complicated and slightly overwhelming to cut and piece. In all honesty, it can be if you don't control the process. The key to quilt-making happiness is to break it down into parts, then it will be relatively simple to put together. Set aside a decent chunk of time for working on this quilt – an afternoon, at least. You don't have to make it all in one go, but I suggest trying to complete a column in one sitting.

The Boro quilt is made up of three different column designs. Column 1 needs to be made three times, and columns 2 and 3 need to be made twice each, making a total of seven columns. Each column is divided into smaller blocks so that it is easier to cut and piece.

Start by planning your fabric placement. You may have scraps of special cloth that need to be used at a certain size, so plan those in first. Mark them onto the diagram on page 102 – or you can trace the diagram with tracing paper and mark your fabric choices on that. Cut these special pieces first and set them aside.

Lay your remaining fabrics out in individual piles near your cutting mat, so that you can choose each piece as you go. You could preplan every fabric placement before you start cutting, but I find that balancing prints, plains and different colours comes naturally to just about everyone. All you need is time to get into the rhythm of choosing and cutting, so don't rush the process.

Clear a space close to your cutting and sewing area so that you can then lay out your pieces as you cut them and see each column forming. With this method, I generally mark the number of each piece on the back with pencil or tailor's chalk, in case I have to stop what I am doing.

Work on one column at a time and each block within that, using the diagram on page 102 as your guide. Starting with column 1, cut all four pieces in block A in the order that they are numbered. Lay them next to each other as you cut them so that you can see a pattern forming. Mix prints and plains as well as colours. Cut striped fabric vertically as well as horizontally (this creates movement in your quilt as well as maximizing the use of the fabric). Some of the pieces have angled edges. For accuracy, cut the fixed measurement first, then mark in the two angled measurements before cutting. When you have cut all of block A, move on to cutting and placing the remaining five blocks. You are now ready to sew your first column.

SEW YOUR QUILT TOP

Start with block A in column 1. Follow the diagram and sew each piece together in the order that you have cut them. Sew A1 to A2. Press the seam. Add A3 and press the seam. Finally, sew A4 to the block. Press the seams and trim any excess thread. Your first block is complete.

Sew the remaining five blocks in column 1 together in the same way, pressing and trimming threads as you go. Follow the diagram and sew the six blocks together to create the completed column.

Repeat this process for the six remaining columns.

Following the diagram, lay all seven columns down and rearrange them if you wish. You may have repeated fabrics in the same position or placed them randomly. This is an opportunity to find the best visual combination. Photograph different compositions so you can compare.

Pin and sew each column together in turn until you have joined all seven. It is important to use pins at this stage to prevent the columns from twisting and stretching. Press the seams, trim the threads, and your quilt top is finished.

SEW YOUR QUILT BACKING

The quilt backing needs to be a minimum of 230 x 230cm. Join your choice of fabric together – in strips, squares or freestyle – until you have a piece the right size. Press the seams, trim any threads, and the backing is complete.

BUILD YOUR QUILT

Put your quilt sandwich together in your preferred way (see page 182). After you have marked any necessary quilting lines, machine- or hand-quilt using your favourite technique (see page 184). Trim the backing and wadding so that the edges are even and your quilt is square. Finally, make and attach the binding (see page 186).

MAKE IT YOURS

Although it is the embodiment of Boro, you don't have to make your quilt in an indigo palette. It is an ideal quilt for including scraps of cloth that are important to you. Use these as the basis for choosing the palette and support fabrics. Reduce the size of the quilt by leaving off one or more columns. You can also rotate or flip the columns, or repeat one column seven times.

STRING

HISTORICALLY, THIS QUILT design was made from the tiniest pieces of cloth – so small that today they would probably be thrown away. String quilts were the ultimate utility quilt – something useful created from almost nothing. They have been around for hundreds of years and were made by rural and frugal communities worldwide. Thriftiness in making is never new; the idea simply seesaws between coming from a real need and a trend.

The String quilt gave women the opportunity to utilize scraps of fabric that were too small for any other purpose. Traditionally, the strips – uneven widths of fabric called 'strings' (hence the name) – were sewn onto a foundation of newspaper or muslin, trimmed and then randomly pieced and sewn together to create a quilt top. It was a matter of luck whether the finished quilt was uniform or completely chaotic in design.

The String quilt is sometimes thought of as a Depression quilt, as this style of quilt was rife during the economic slump of the early twentieth century. Many rural women lived below the breadline but still needed to provide warmth for their families. Each quilter found their own style of String quilt – there were no rules, patterns, set sizes or plans, as speed was the most important factor. The women cut 'strings' from used, old and new fabrics of any type. No matter whether they were fat or thin, long or short, straight or on the bias, the strips were sewn together and trimmed as necessary. An old quilt or blanket was used as wadding, and then the quilts were roughly stitched or tied to finish. Job done.

Of the thousands of String quilts created, very few have survived. As they were made as utilitarian objects, most would have been used until they were threadbare and then recycled. Quilt collectors generally overlooked those that survived, as they looked clumsy and hastily made, which I am sure is now a matter of regret.

The String quilt concept was adopted by the Gee's Bend and Amish quilting communities. Both groups understood the need that the String quilt fulfilled, as well as the beauty of them. These quilts are, of course, now highly revered.

I am passionate about doing rather than perfecting. If we had no choice, we would make quilts with whatever we had, so I urge you to try a String quilt and use fabric you already have. They are simple, quick and enchanting in their naïve finish. If you need just one more reason to create a String quilt – they work.

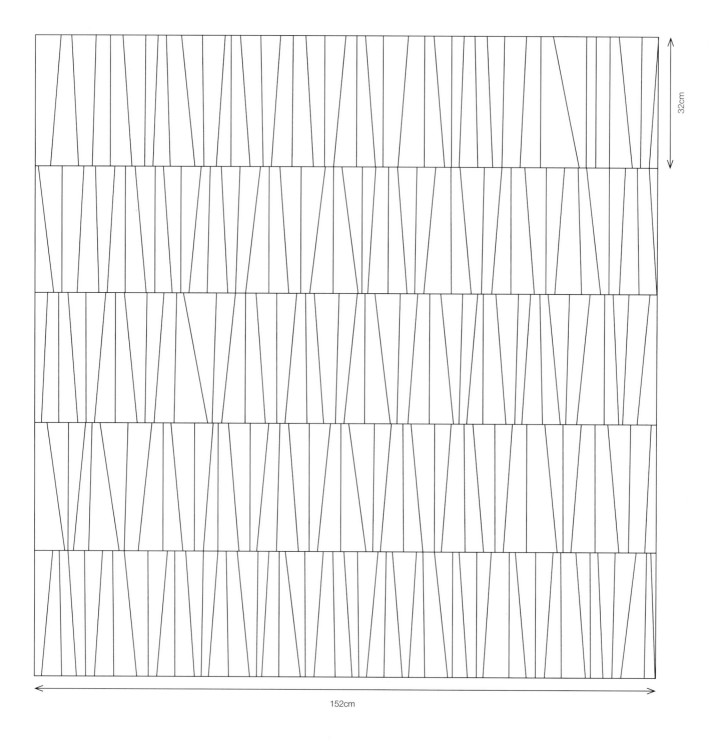

32cm

152cm

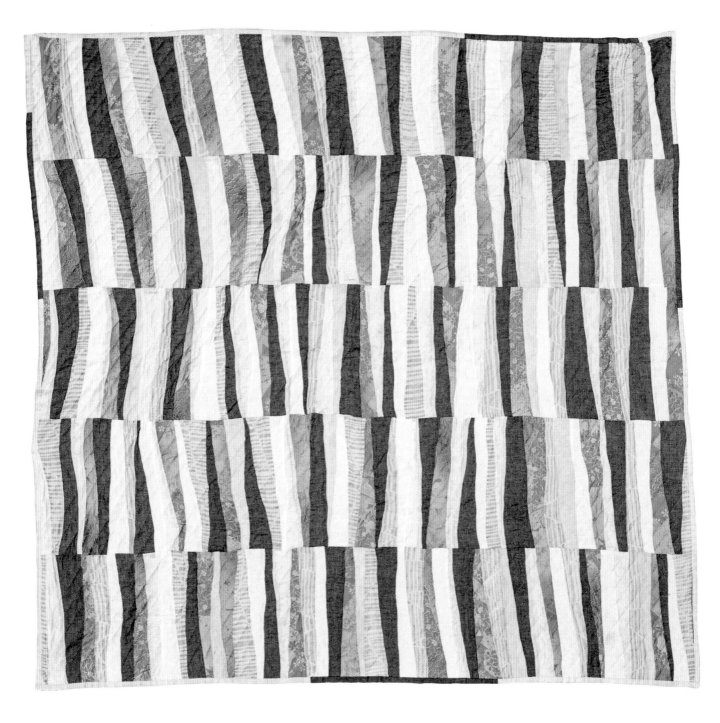

'The fabric is simply cut into uneven widths, or "strings", and then randomly pieced together to form blocks.'

QUILT SIZE

150 x 150cm when trimmed and bound. All seam allowances are 1cm and are already built into the cutting sizes.

QUILT TOP

You will need approximately 4–5m of fabric. This is a perfect quilt design to use up scraps from other quilts or sewing projects, but you can, of course, buy something new or repurpose stash or clothing. The only restriction is that each piece of fabric has to be a minimum of 34cm in length.

I used a very simple mixture of ivory khadi and canvas cottons, natural and white linen, and the silk lining from two kimonos. Although the colour palette is subtle, the quilt has a wonderful mix of textures and sheen.

QUILT BACKING

You will need approximately 3.5–4m of fabric. The finished size should be at least 170 x 170cm, so you can also piece fabric leftovers to make the quilt backing, or use fabric from a bolt of cloth.

BINDING

You will need approximately 0.5m of fabric. You can use scraps from the quilt top if you have any left over, or use the binding as an opportunity to introduce a new fabric.

I used the leftover scraps from the quilt top so that the binding practically disappeared within the design.

OTHER MATERIALS

WADDING of your choice, 170 x 170cm.
SEWING THREAD 100 per cent cotton all-purpose thread is best, in a neutral colour.
QUILTING THREAD 100 per cent cotton quilting thread in a colour of your choice.

CUT YOUR FABRIC

This is an astonishingly simple (and satisfying) quilt to cut. You will cut all of your fabric before you start sewing and you don't need to preplan any fabric placement.

Gather your chosen fabrics together and press. Select your first cloth and cut it into 34cm lengths – the pieces can be any width. Then you need to cut each piece into individual strips, or 'strings'. Using your rotary cutter and quilter's ruler, cut the fabric into irregular widths – these can be angled (wide to thin, or thin to wide) or straight up and down. Look at the diagram on page 108 to understand the cutting technique. This is one of the few quilt designs where you don't need to measure. You will soon fall into a natural rhythm and will find cutting in this way is super-fast.

Once you have cut all of one fabric, put it to one side and cut the rest of your fabric using the same technique. You may have cut more or less than you need, but you can always use the excess to start another quilt, or add in more fabrics if you run out.

Place each fabric in its own pile or put them in labelled envelopes to keep them under control. This is a good idea if you are not going to finish the quilt in one sitting.

You are ready to sew the quilt together.

SEW YOUR QUILT TOP

From your individual fabric piles or envelopes, choose your first two pieces and sew them right sides together along one long edge. If you are joining two irregular or wedge-shaped pieces, make sure that the wide end of one is sewn to the thin end of the other. This ensures that you are creating a straight block rather than curving off into a circle. Continue adding pieces in an order that you like until your first row is 155cm long. Don't worry about drawing evenly from each of the different fabrics – again, you will find a natural rhythm that is visually pleasing. Your block may look a little off-kilter at times, but the extra fabric allowance in the length of the strips will allow you to trim your block to the right size, with straight edges, before you sew the quilt top together.

Once your first strip is complete, press it on both sides, remove any excess threads and trim it to 32 x 152cm.

Repeat this for the remaining four blocks, so that you have five completed rows in total.

Lay the five rows down next to each other and move them around to create an order that you like. You can flip the direction of the rows as well as change the order of them. Remember to use your phone, camera or tablet to record compositions you like. Pin and sew each row

'The String quilt has no rules, patterns or plans, and you can use old, new or repurposed fabric of any type.'

together, being careful not to stretch them. To ensure straight rows, simply rotate your work by 180° each time you stitch two of the rows together.

Press all the seams and trim away any excess sewing thread. Your quilt top is complete.

SEW YOUR QUILT BACKING

Your quilt backing needs to be a minimum of 170 x 170cm. You may have a piece of fabric or a lovely vintage sheet that is already that size. If not, join your choice of fabric together until you have a backing the right size. Press all the seams, trim away any excess threads, and your quilt backing is finished.

BUILD YOUR QUILT

Put your quilt sandwich together in your preferred way (see page 182). After you have marked any necessary quilting lines, machine- or hand-quilt using your favourite technique (see page 184). Trim the backing and wadding so that the edges are even and your quilt is square. Finally, make and attach your binding (see page 186).

MAKE IT YOURS

This quilt can be any size – from cot to super-king. The bigger the quilt, the more care you need to take to ensure straight rows, but you can always make a larger number of smaller blocks, which you then join together. The String quilt is perfect for using up leftovers from other projects and is a fantastic beginner's quilt to get you started.

WELSH BARS

TALES OF BEAUTY and creativity triumphing over poverty and necessity are endemic in most quilting tribes. When a quilt was needed, it was made – with whatever was available. Of course, there were also the refined quilts for the aristocracy, and these are also prevalent in almost every quilting country. The Welsh quilting community worked slightly differently from most, in that quilt-making was a profession as well as a pastime. Their quilting styles were similar to North Country quilts – both communities made Wholecloth, Frame, Bars and Strippy quilts – but Welsh quilt-making was an industry and a respected way of earning an income, which is probably why we have so many historical examples to draw from.

Welsh quilts had their own idiosyncratic style, but, because most were professionally made, they were also of a very high standard. It was customary to employ a quilter if you wanted a beautifully stitched quilt. Housewives did make their own, but these were much 'rougher' and utilitarian in finish; they were used until they wore out, so there are very few remaining, whereas quilts that were paid for were looked after and kept for best. Being a 'travelling quilter' was a fairly respectable profession. Skilled needleworkers would travel the country, often with an apprentice in tow. When they received a commission, they would stay with the family while stitching the quilt. This would take between two and three weeks, which seems very quick when you consider the elaborate stitching involved.

Welsh quilting has been traced back to the sixteenth century, but these examples were mainly found in the homes of the wealthy. It was several hundred years before the rural and mining communities engaged wholeheartedly in quilt-making. Their early quilts were purely serviceable items, often made from heavy wool with an old blanket as the middle layer. Commercially made fabric was very expensive, so the humble relied on homespun woollen cloth to make their quilts. Once cotton became cheaper, quilting became widespread as both a pastime and a source of income.

Most of the mining and rural communities were isolated, so their quilts soon developed a signature look. There was very little outside influence, until returning families brought quilts back with them from America. Fabrics were often plain and used in striking combinations, with intricate quilting patterns that made them so highly sought-after.

My quilt design is a slightly more complex version of the simple Welsh Bars quilt. I wanted to keep the idea of the uncomplicated vertical lines, but added extra blocks to create movement, pattern and colour. It is still a very easy quilt to cut and piece, but I think it gives you room to add in small and special scraps of fabric to really personalize it.

			7						19	
			8						20	
				10					21	
				11	13	14				22
						15				23
	4	6					18			
	5									
1						16				
2						17				
3										
			12							
			9							

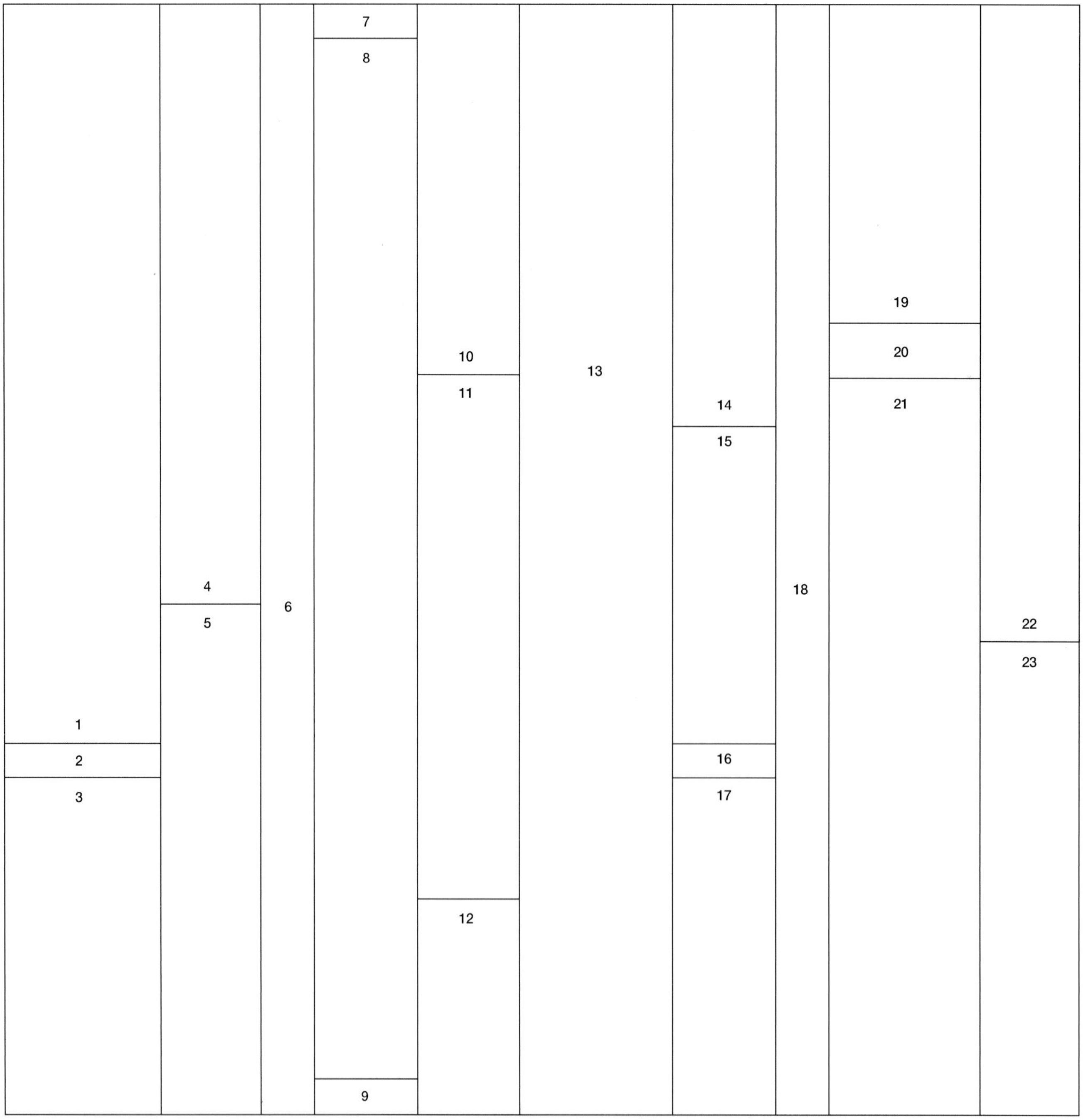

1 32 x 142cm	**13** 32 x 212cm
2 32 x 8cm	**14** 22 x 82cm
3 32 x 66cm	**15** 22 x 62cm
4 22 x 116cm	**16** 22 x 8cm
5 22 x 98cm	**17** 22 x 66cm
6 12 x 212cm	**18** 12 x 212cm
7 22 x 8cm	**19** 32 x 62cm
8 22 x 200cm	**20** 32 x 12cm
9 22 x 8cm	**21** 32 x 142cm
10 22 x 72cm	**22** 22 x 122cm
11 22 x 102cm	**23** 22 x 92cm
12 22 x 42cm	

'The beauty of this quilt lies in its effortlessness and use of humble cloth, but the design is also ideal for including special scraps of fabric.'

QUILT SIZE

210 x 210cm when trimmed and bound. All seam allowances are 1cm and are already built into the cutting sizes.

QUILT TOP

You will need approximately 5–6m of fabric. This is a very uncomplicated (and therefore suitably rewarding) quilt to create. It is merely six or seven different fabrics cut and sewn into large strips. Your effort should be put into the fabric choice and the quilting, as this will make the quilt greater than the sum of its parts.

Because most of the pieces are large, it is important to preplan where each fabric will be positioned. Trace off the diagram on page 114 and draw or colour in your choices. You can then very easily work out how much you will need of each fabric.

This was a lovely and very peaceful quilt to put together. I started with a pale blue and grey Japanese kimono silk and an indigo block-printed cotton, also from Japan. I added two pale blue woven cottons and then drew from my stash of lovely plains.

QUILT BACKING

You will need approximately 5m of cloth. The finished size should be at least 230 x 230cm, so you can also use fabric leftovers to make the backing, or pick something to contrast with the quilt top.

BINDING

You will need approximately 0.5m of fabric. You can use scraps from the quilt top if you have any left over, or use the binding as an opportunity to introduce a new fabric.

I used ivory cotton in keeping with the calm feel of the quilt.

OTHER MATERIALS

WADDING of your choice, 230 x 230cm.
SEWING THREAD 100 per cent cotton all-purpose thread is best, in a neutral colour.
QUILTING THREAD 100 per cent cotton quilting thread in a colour of your choice.

CUT YOUR FABRIC

Clear a large space close to your cutting and sewing area. You can then lay down the pieces as you cut them in order to see the quilt forming. This gives you a chance to change the layout if it doesn't look quite as you had imagined.

Use the diagram on page 114 as your cutting guide. You don't have to start at number 1, just pick one of your fabrics and cut all the pieces from that cloth. Mark the number on the back and position them according to the diagram. Once you have cut all 23 pieces, you are ready to sew.

SEW YOUR QUILT TOP

Piecing this quilt top shouldn't take more than one to two hours, so try to set aside enough time to complete it in one sitting. This quilt is constructed like one very large block, so you will piece it together in this way.

Following the diagram, sew the pieces together in number order. Sew 1 to 2, then join 3 to 2. Press the seams and cut away excess threads. Sew 4 to 5, and press. Then pin and sew this to 1/2/3. Pin long seams to avoid the fabric stretching, and change the direction of sewing by 180° to ensure the seams don't curve (see page 156).

Continue sewing, pressing and trimming until you have joined all 23 pieces. Give it one final press and trim, and your quilt top is finished.

SEW YOUR QUILT BACKING

Your quilt backing needs to be a minimum of 230 x 230cm. Join your choice of fabric together until you have a backing the right size. Press all the seams and trim away any excess threads. Your quilt backing is now complete.

BUILD YOUR QUILT

Put your quilt sandwich together in your preferred way (see page 182). After you have marked any necessary quilting lines, machine- or hand-quilt using your favourite technique (see page 184). Trim the backing and wadding so that the edges are even and your quilt is square. Finally, make and attach your binding (see page 186).

MAKE IT YOURS

This is a great quilt to practise adjusting designs. For example, if you have fabrics that you would like to use for this design that aren't the right size, you can move the cutting lines on any of the pieces to make them shorter or skinnier. It is easy to make the quilt smaller or larger, and you could even use this design to create a quilt backing on one of the more complicated designs. You will just need to add an extra 20cm to the width and length, but it would give you a completely reversible quilt – genius.

ENGLISH PIECING

THERE IS A SIMPLE restorative pleasure in sewing by hand. You just need yourself, some fabric, a needle and thread – and a little concentration. No gadgets, no noise, nothing else.

English paper piecing is sewn completely by hand and is one of the first recorded quilt-making techniques. Some English quilts date back to the 1770s and the oldest American version dates back to about 1810. In the eighteenth century the importation of Indian cotton and chintz to England and France was restricted, which meant that fabric became very precious and every piece really had to count. The method of English paper piecing allowed every scrap to be used and all types of fabric – silk and velvet, as well as cotton – were gathered to create these tactile treasures. Women created a wide variety of quilts, table coverings, throws and cushion covers from the tiny hexagons, as there really was no limit to the designs they could create. As a sewing technique, it was a perfect teaching device for young girls. Both simple and portable, it was an extremely respectable pastime to illustrate stitching prowess.

Although usually in hexagon form, English piecing also used other tessellating geometric shapes to create quilts, including diamonds, octagons and triangles, to great effect. These shapes provided an easy way of creating complex geometric patterns, such as Tumbling Blocks and Flower Garden, which are some of the most recognized quilt designs of all. This style of patchwork was known as an all-over design, rather than the latterly more common frame or block designs, and every piece had to be considered within the overall design of the quilt. Although paper-pieced quilts were simple to execute, they required great patience. The great number of pieces in the quilt – often thousands – and their small size became a matter of pride for early quilters.

Paper templates were used as fabric stabilizers to ensure accuracy when hand-sewing the complex angles together. English pieced quilts were not padded or quilted, so the paper templates were often left in the quilt for additional insulation and to ensure that the shapes stayed flat. The templates themselves are often important pieces of history – plain paper was scarce, so they were usually cut from old letters, newspapers, bills or journals. Thus we can catch a glimpse of the lives of the makers, not only through their fabric and design choices, but also through their letters and other written records.

I would love to make a whole quilt from English pieced hexagons – and one day, in the very distant future, I will. I love the handmade aspect of this technique as much as using complex shapes to such fantastically simple effect. A few rows of hexagons are achievable for all and offer a wonderful way to use the tiniest of scraps for a strikingly graphic result.

Finished quilt top measures: 152 x 152cm

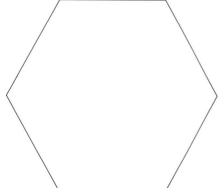

Trace the hexagon shape
to create your template.

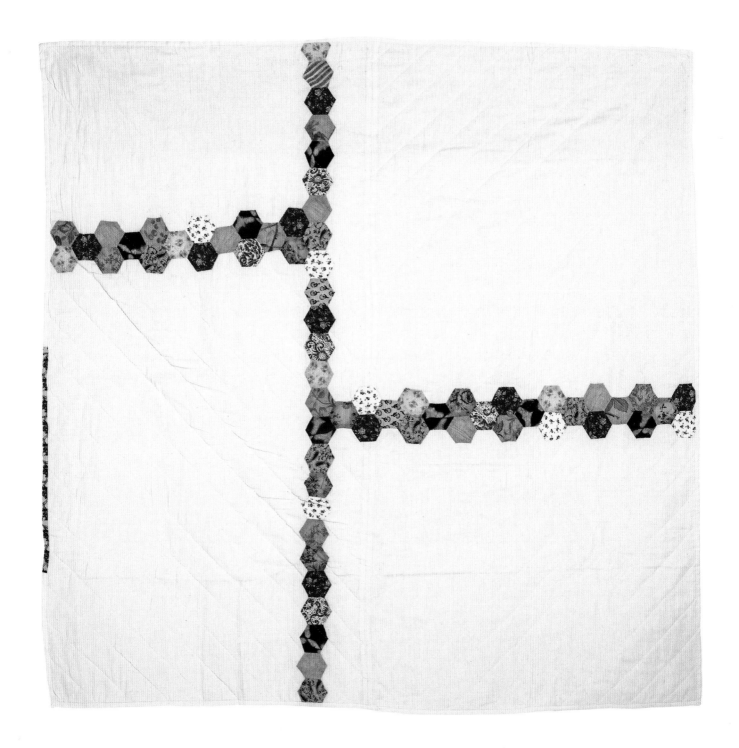

'English piecing is a wonderful, traditional technique for using up the tiniest scraps of fabric, to striking and graphic effect.'

QUILT SIZE
150 x 150cm when trimmed and bound. All seam allowances are 1cm and are included in the cutting sizes.

QUILT TOP
Your quilt top requires a base cloth with a finished size of 152 x 152cm. Once you have chosen your fabric for this, you can easily work out the amount you need by the width of the fabric you are buying. For example, if you choose a wide fabric, you will need only one length at 155cm. If you are buying standard-width fabric, then you will need 310cm. You will have wastage from this but you can use it on the backing and binding, or for other projects.

You will also need approximately 0.5m of fabric scraps for your hexagons; each scrap needs to be a minimum of 10 x 10cm square.

I used a fine organic cotton as my base cloth and a selection of Indian and French block-printed cottons in reds, natural tones and shades of indigo for my hand-stitched pieces. I wanted to make this quilt appealing for a little girl, but I also wanted it to be something that she would still love once she had grown out of the customary pink phase.

QUILT BACKING
You will need approximately 2.5m of fabric. The finished size should be at least 170 x 170cm, so you can use any fabric that is left over from the front base cloth to make the backing, or quickly freestyle some other fabric pieces of your choice together to the required size.

I did just that, piecing lemon, indigo and vintage printed cotton together to create a graphic backing.

BINDING
You will need approximately 0.5m of fabric. You can use scraps from the quilt top if you have any left over, or use the binding as an opportunity to introduce a new fabric.

I bound my quilt with a mixture of plain ivory cotton and one of the block-printed cottons – just because I had some left over and I thought it would look fun.

OTHER MATERIALS
WADDING of your choice, 170 x 170cm.
SEWING THREAD 100 per cent cotton all-purpose thread is best, in a neutral colour.
QUILTING THREAD 100 per cent cotton quilting thread in a colour of your choice.
TEMPLATE PAPER such as baking paper or tracing paper, and a pencil.

CUT YOUR FABRIC
Start by tracing the hexagon on page 122. I generally use baking paper, as it is easy to sew through and there is always some in the kitchen drawer. You need to cut out 66 hexagons, so you can either trace the hexagon 66 times, or create a cardboard template that you can then draw around (see page 179).

Press all your scrap fabrics and, with the fabric wrong side up, pin the paper templates to them. Make sure that one edge of each template is sitting on the straight grain of the fabric.

Using a ruler and pencil, draw a 1cm seam allowance around the outside of the paper templates. Cut out all of your fabric hexagons using scissors or a rotary cutter.

Turn the seam allowance to the wrong side over the edge of the template. Hand-sew tacking stitches along each side to hold it in place, folding the corners neatly and stitching through the folds to keep the corners sharp. Repeat for the remaining 65 templates. This is a very portable sewing technique, so you can easily do it while watching television or travelling.

SEW YOUR QUILT TOP
To join the hexagons into one long block, follow the shape on the diagram on page 122. Stitch the pieces together using the following technique:

Place two shapes with right sides together. Knot your thread and hand-stitch two edges together using very small stitches. Do not sew through the paper. Once you have reached the end, backstitch over the last few stitches and knot. Cut the thread.

Continue to add hexagons in one row until you have joined 25 together. Your central block is complete.

Repeat this technique for the side blocks, taking care to stagger the hexagons in rows of 1/2/1/2, and so on. The left-hand block is made up of 17 hexagons and the right-hand block 24.

Once you have completed these, stitch them to the central block. The left block is joined to the central block at pieces 7/8/9 and the right block is joined at 14/15.

Join your base cloth fabric together until you have a piece measuring 152 x 152cm. Press this well. Place your base cloth right side up on a clean surface – I find a table is best for this quilt – and use masking tape around the edges to keep it straight and taut. Steam press your hexagon blocks so that the edges are crisp.

Lay the hexagon block down on the base cloth, matching the ends to the edges of the base cloth. Use the diagram for guidance. Use a long metal ruler and your quilter's ruler to ensure that the block stays straight.

Start at the top of the quilt and remove the tacking stitches and paper template from the first hexagon. Pin the edges of the fabric hexagon to the base cloth. Continue removing the tacking stitches and templates and pinning the hexagons to the base cloth. Use your rulers to check that the block stays aligned as you work. This is fiddly, but it will be easier if you have pressed the block well.

Once you have pinned the whole block to the base cloth, simply slipstitch the hexagons in place, using tiny (as invisible as possible) stitches. That's it – your quilt top is finished.

SEW YOUR QUILT BACKING

Your quilt backing needs to be a minimum of 170 x 170cm. Simply join your choice of fabric together until you have a backing the right size. Press all the seams, trim away any excess threads, and your backing is complete.

BUILD YOUR QUILT

Put your quilt sandwich together in your preferred way (see page 182). After you have marked any necessary quilting lines, machine- or hand-quilt using your favourite technique (see page 184). Trim the backing and wadding so that the edges are even and your quilt is square. Finally, make and attach your binding (see page 186).

'It is a rare delight when we get to sit quietly and make with our hands, but we always feel all the better for giving ourselves the time.'

MAKE IT YOURS

Once you understand the principle of the English piecing technique, you can create your own design, increase the size of the hexagons, or increase or decrease the size of the quilt top itself. As most of this quilt is hand-stitched, you can make a large number of hexagons and then decide on your design when you are ready. You could, of course, make a whole quilt out of these hexagons. This would be a long-term commitment but with a very beautiful result.

STRIPPY

A STRIPPY QUILT may very well be one of the first quilts you ever made (or are about to make). They are very simple to cut and piece, look delightful and reward the maker with a finished quilt top in a relative jiffy. A Strippy quilt is exactly what its name suggests: long strips of cloth sewn together in rows to create a quilt top. Strippy layouts are created by placing quilt blocks in either horizontal or vertical rows. It is a quilt style that is still popular with modern and traditional quilters around the world. The wide variety of fabrics available today means that Strippy quilts can be as plain or as patterned as the maker wishes, so the effort is focused on the visual aspect of the design, rather than its construction.

Strippy quilts were originally popular between 1860 and 1930 in Wales and the north of England. As they were easy to make, they were often used as utilitarian quilts, rather than being saved for 'best'. These quilts were simply made up of bars or strips in a width that suited the maker. The busy textile industry in England at this time meant that cotton fabrics were available and not too expensive for the average maker to use in such large pieces. The strips of plain cloth provided an opportunity for the maker to really show their stitching ability and let their stitches sing out. The Strippy quilt design travelled to America, where the Amish community embraced the simplicity of the design and adjusted its composition to suit their environment. There are also versions of Strippy quilts within Gee's Bend designs – both old and new. It seems that communities who valued natural design embraced the idea of a Strippy quilt.

I think of Strippy quilts as the 'jeans and T-shirts' of the quilt world. Not fancy, but extremely useful and easy in every sense. I imagine they would have provided light relief for the makers from some of the more complicated quilting techniques.

There are three quilts in this book based on a strip method, all of which have produced very different results. The Welsh Bars quilt (see page 112); this narrower, more modern Strippy quilt; and the Amish Sawtooth quilt (see page 60). They are all born from the original Welsh and North Country Strippy quilts, yet provide a number of starting points from a very simple premise.

Finished quilt top measures: 222 x 222cm

A 1a 2a 3a 4a 5a
B 1b 2b 3b 4b 5b
C 1c 2c 3c 4c 5c
D 1d 2d 3d 4d 5d
A 1a 2a 3a 4a 5a
B 1b 2b 3b 4b 5b
C 1c 2c 3c 4c 5c
D 1d 2d 3d 4d 5d
A 1a 2a 3a 4a 5a
B 1b 2b 3b 4b 5b
C 1c 2c 3c 4c 5c
D 1d 2d 3d 4d 5d
A 1a 2a 3a 4a 5a
B 1b 2b 3b 4b 5b
C 1c 2c 3c 4c 5c
D 1d 2d 3d 4d 5d
A 1a 2a 3a 4a 5a
B 1b 2b 3b 4b 5b
C 1c 2c 3c 4c 5c
D 1d 2d 3d 4d 5d
A 1a 2a 3a 4a 5a
B 1b 2b 3b 4b 5b
C 1c 2c 3c 4c 5c
D 1d 2d 3d 4d 5d
A 1a 2a 3a 4a 5a
B 1b 2b 3b 4b 5b
C 1c 2c 3c 4c 5c
D 1d 2d 3d 4d 5d
A 1a 2a 3a 4a 5a
B 1b 2b 3b 4b 5b
C 1c 2c 3c 4c 5c
D 1d 2d 3d 4d 5d
A 1a 2a 3a 4a 5a
B 1b 2b 3b 4b 5b
C 1c 2c 3c 4c 5c
D 1d 2d 3d 4d 5d
A 1a 2a 3a 4a 5a
B 1b 2b 3b 4b 5b
C 1c 2c 3c 4c 5c
D 1d 2d 3d 4d 5d
A 1a 2a 3a 4a 5a
B 1b 2b 3b 4b 5b
C 1c 2c 3c 4c 5c
D 1d 2d 3d 4d 5d

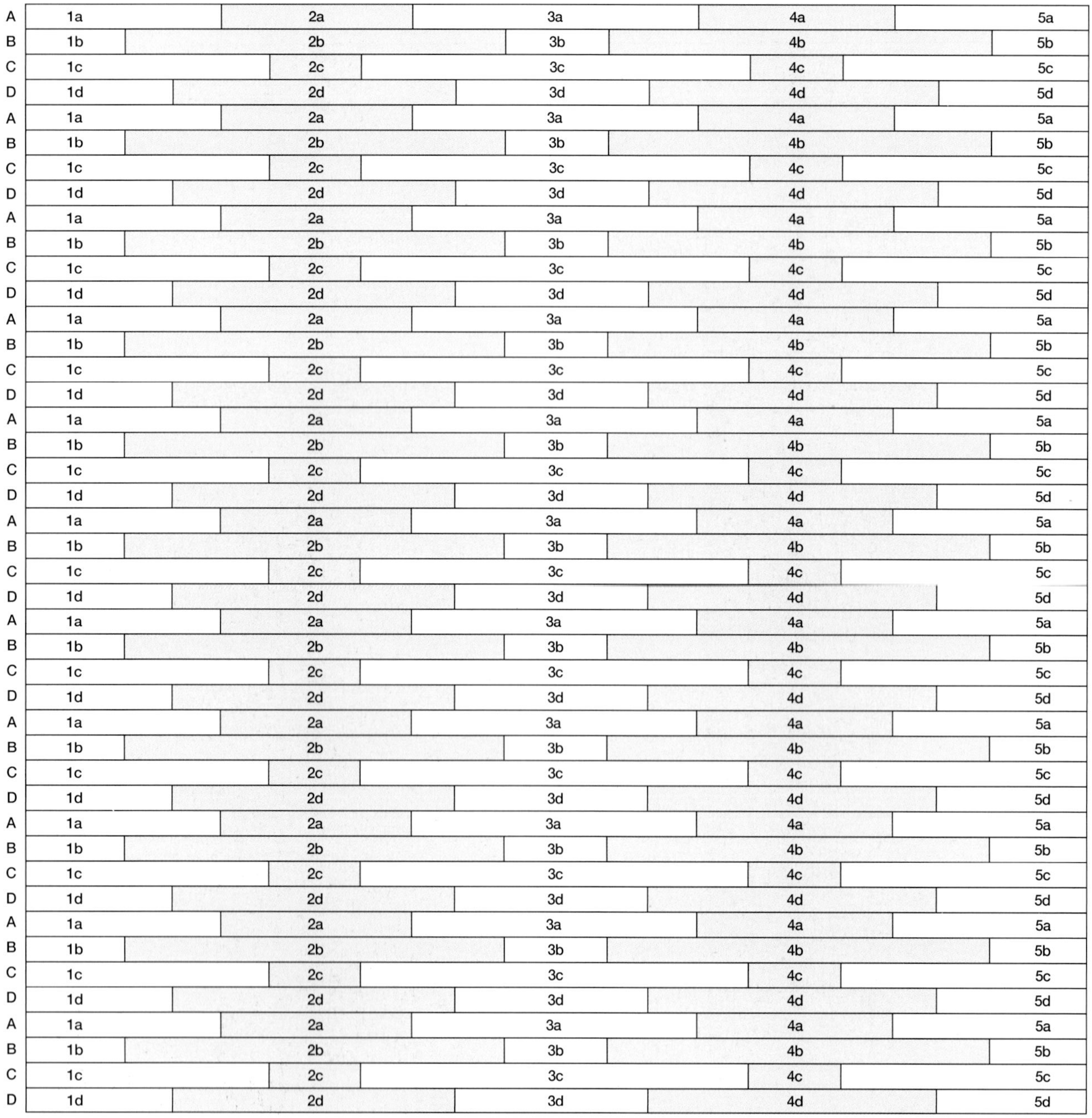

Fabric 1 (ivory cotton)
1a cut 11 of 42 x 7cm
1b cut 11 of 22 x 7cm
1c cut 11 of 52 x 7cm
1d cut 11 of 32 x 7cm

Fabric 2 (I have used a different fabric for each of the four rows)
2a cut 11 of 42 x 7cm
2b cut 11 of 82 x 7cm
2c cut 11 of 22 x 7cm
2d cut 11 of 62 x 7cm

Fabric 3 (ivory cotton)
3a cut 11 of 62 x 7cm
3b cut 11 of 22 x 7cm
3c cut 11 of 82 x 7cm
3d cut 11 of 42 x 7cm

Fabric 4 (I have used a different fabric for each of the four rows)
4a cut 11 of 42 x 7cm
4b cut 11 of 82 x 7cm
4c cut 11 of 22 x 7cm
4d cut 11 of 62 x 7cm

Fabric 5 (ivory cotton)
5a cut 11 of 42 x 7cm
5b cut 11 of 22 x 7cm
5c cut 11 of 52 x 7cm
5d cut 11 of 32 x 7cm

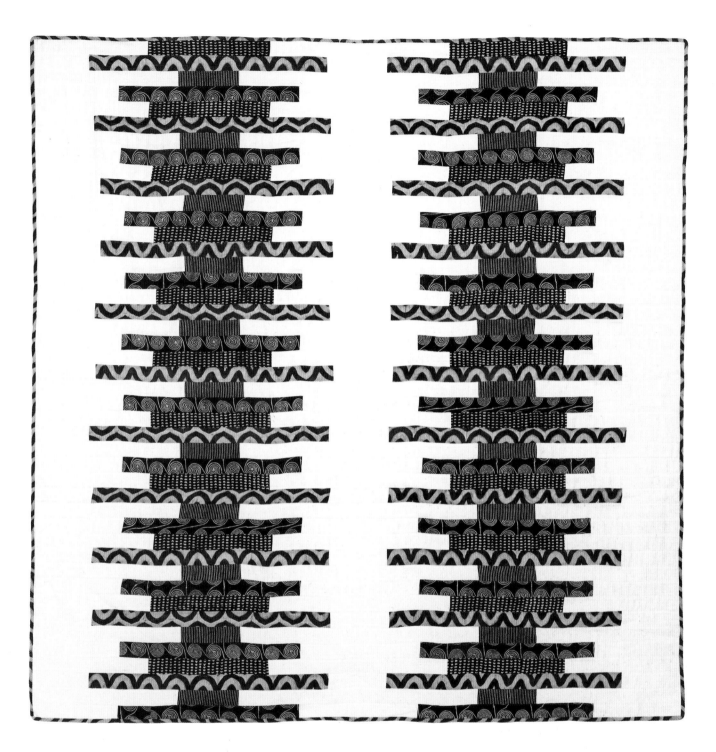

'Strippy quilts are simply long
strips of cloth, in a width of
your choice, sewn together in
vertical or horizontal rows.'

QUILT SIZE

220 x 220cm when trimmed and bound. All seam allowances are 1cm and are already built into the cutting sizes.

QUILT TOP

These are the fabric quantities you need in order to make the quilt top with five different fabrics, but it should be relatively easy to work out what you need if you would like to use a different number of fabrics.
Fabric 1: 3.5m (ivory)
Fabric 2: 0.8m
Fabric 3: 1.6m
Fabric 4: 0.4m
Fabric 5: 1.6m

QUILT BACKING

You will need approximately 5m of fabric. The finished size should be 240 x 240cm, so you can use fabric leftovers or fabric from a bolt of cloth.
I simply used more of the ivory cotton to make my quilt backing.

BINDING

You will need approximately 0.5m of fabric. You can use scraps from the quilt top if you have any left over, or use the binding as an opportunity to introduce a new fabric.
I used scraps of one of the indigo fabrics to bind my quilt so that the indigo blocks within the quilt top felt 'contained'.

OTHER MATERIALS

WADDING of your choice, 240 x 240cm.
SEWING THREAD 100 per cent cotton all-purpose thread is best, in a neutral colour.
QUILTING THREAD 100 per cent cotton quilting thread in a colour of your choice.

CUT YOUR FABRIC

Look at the diagram and photograph on pages 128–9 to see how the quilt fits together and then plan your fabric choices. If it helps, trace off the diagram and draw in your fabric placement.

This quilt is relatively simple to cut and sew, but because each piece of fabric is long and thin, it is easy to lose them and you can definitely get confused. It is a good idea to clear a space large enough to lay the quilt out as you are making it. Push the furniture against the wall or set yourself up in a bedroom so that you can lay each strip of fabric down on the bed in the correct order as you work.

My version of this quilt is made up of four different indigo cottons for blocks 2 and 4, and one ivory khadi cotton for blocks 1, 3 and 5. The instructions are therefore based on using five fabrics, but you can use as many different fabrics as you want.

Mark the outside of 20 envelopes with the number of each cutting piece – 1a, 3d, and so on. As you cut the required number of each piece, put them inside the envelope until you are ready to start sewing. You may have enough time to cut out only part of your quilt in one go, so this method keeps everything exactly where you need it and prevents confusion.

Following the diagram and cutting guide on page 128, cut out all of your strips. Now you are ready to sew.

SEW YOUR QUILT TOP

Line up your envelopes with your cut pieces placed on top. Make sure you have a clear area that is bigger than the quilt so that you see the quilt building as you make it.

The quilt is made up of 11 sets of 4 rows (A, B, C, D) – so 44 rows in total.

Start with the first row A and follow the diagram to sew the required pieces together, end to end, in the right order. Sew 1a to 2a, then add 3a, 4a and 5a. If you are using lots of different fabrics, take your time to choose them to get a balance that you like the look of. Press all the seams and trim off any excess thread. Lay the first row down where you can see it.

Repeat this for row B – sew 1b to 2b, then add 3b, 4b and 5b in turn. Press all the seams, trim off any excess sewing thread and lay this row below row A.

Repeat this for row C – joining 1c to 2c, then 3c, 4c and 5c in turn. Press all the seams, trim off any excess sewing thread and lay this row below row B.

To finish your first group of four rows, sew row D together in the same way – sew 1d to 2d, then add 3d, 4d and 5d in turn. Press the seams, trim off the threads and lay this row below row C.

Sew these four rows together to create your first group. Pin and sew row A to row B, making sure the centre of each strip is matched and being careful not to stretch the fabric. Pin and sew row C to the other edge of row B. Pin

and sew row D to the other edge of row C. Press all the seams and trim away any excess sewing thread. You have now completed your first group of four rows.

Repeat this 10 times. You will then have 11 blocks.

Place the 11 blocks in an order that you like. If you have repeated fabrics, as I have, then this will be a fairly rapid task. If you have used lots of different fabrics, it may take a little longer. Use your camera, phone or tablet to take pictures of alternative layouts. Once you have decided on an order, pin and sew each section together, working from the top of the quilt down. Press all the seams, trim away any excess thread, and your quilt top is finished.

SEW YOUR QUILT BACKING

Your quilt backing needs to be a minimum of 240 x 240cm. You may have fabric already that size. If not, join your choice of fabric together until you have a backing the correct size. Press all the seams, trim away any excess thread, and your quilt backing is complete.

BUILD YOUR QUILT

Put your quilt sandwich together in your preferred way (see page 182). After you have marked any necessary quilting lines, machine- or hand-quilt using your favourite technique (see page 184). Trim the backing and wadding so that the edges are even and your quilt is square. Finally, make and attach your binding (see page 186).

MAKE IT YOURS

My palette and choice of fabrics are extremely uniform, as my plan was to see two vertical indigo blocks framed within ivory cotton. You could reverse the design and have the patterned blocks as plain and the plain as patterned; you could use 50 different fabrics or just two.

LOG CABIN

THE LOG CABIN is one of the most loved and recognizable quilt designs of all time. They are in plentiful supply in markets and antique stores in both English villages and American towns. Although the Log Cabin is considered an American design, it was one of the key quilt patterns brought back to Britain with returning immigrants, and then dispersed around the world. Log Cabin quilts have always been made from a huge variety of fabrics, so embody the 'make-do-and-mend' philosophy perfectly. The clever use of colour and pattern can create an almost endless array of configurations. In all its guises, it was, and still is, one of the most popular quilt designs.

The Log Cabin dates back to the Civil War period in America (1861–5), when many quilts were sewn and raffled to raise money, initially for the abolition of slavery and latterly for the troops. The quilt is often connected to Abraham Lincoln, as some believe its design was a tribute to his childhood home, a one-room log cabin in Kentucky. Whether this story is true, the Log Cabin is known as the design that reflects the pioneering spirit and principal values of America.

It is difficult to be entirely accurate on the history of any quilt design. Perhaps folklore is more interesting than fact, or it may be that there was a need to attach meaning to these handcrafted possessions. However accurate the story, we know that this was a challenging period for women in America. The life of a pioneer was hard and women had little, if any, influence on the decisions made about their lives. Creating quilts was often the only way to express their thoughts, beliefs and passions, and their work became a visual manifestation of those convictions and emotions.

The earliest Log Cabin quilts were hand-pieced using strips of fabrics around a central square. Traditionally, one half was made with dark fabrics and the other half with light. A red central square symbolized the hearth of home, while a yellow one meant a welcoming light in the window. Some say quilts with black centre squares were used as a 'Stop' sign for slaves escaping through the Underground Railroad movement. Log Cabin quilts were easy and versatile to piece. Women could easily adjust the initial design to reflect their location, lifestyle and views. White House Steps, Streak of Lightening, Barn Raising, and Sunshine and Shadows are just some of the hundreds of name and pattern variations, which were all created by the adroit arrangement of contrasting colours. Because of their strong construction, Log Cabin quilts were rarely quilted, but instead were knotted together or tufted.

In the spirit of the quilt's origins, I wanted to stick to basics and make a small quilt of 16 simply pieced blocks. Precision is important, but if that isn't your strong suit, you could always marry the traditional Log Cabin with the Gee's Bend version to create yet another new quilt design. Why not?

Individual Log Cabin block: make 16

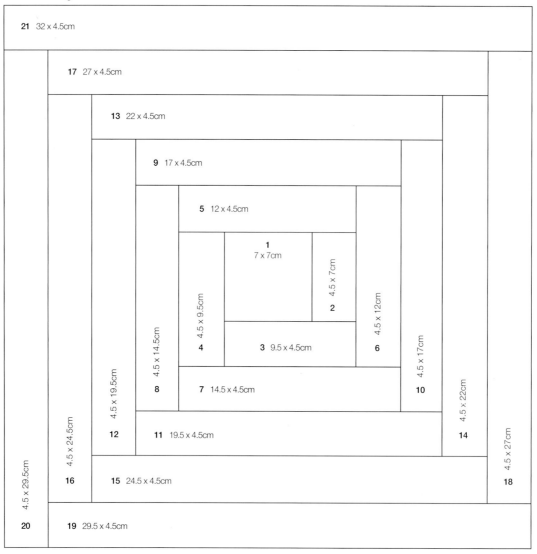

Quilt layout comprising 16 Log Cabin blocks

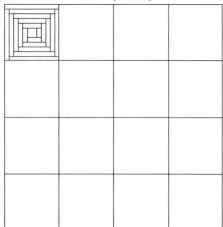

Fabric A (ivory calico)
Press the fabric well.
First cut it into 4.5cm
strips, then cut:
2   16 of 4.5 x 7cm
3   16 of 9.5 x 4.5cm
6   16 of 4.5 x 12cm
7   16 of 14.5 x 4.5cm
10 16 of 4.5 x 17cm
11 16 of 19.5 x 4.5cm
14 16 of 4.5 x 22cm
15 16 of 24.5 x 4.5cm
18 16 of 4.5 x 27cm
19 16 of 29.5 x 4.5cm

Fabric B (ivory and
pink vintage silk)
Choose your fabric for
the centre squares and
press it well, then cut:
1   16 of 7 x 7cm

Fabric C (mix of blue
Japanese kimono silks)
Press the fabric well.
First cut it into 4.5cm
strips, then cut:
4   16 of 4.5 x 9.5cm
5   16 of 12 x 4.5cm
8   16 of 4.5 x 14.5cm
9   16 of 17 x 4.5cm
12 16 of 4.5 x 19.5cm
13 16 of 22 x 4.5cm
16 16 of 4.5 x 24.5cm
17 16 of 27 x 4.5cm
20 16 of 4.5 x 29.5cm
21 16 of 32 x 4.5cm

'The Log Cabin is a very simple quilt to sew. As you build each block, you are simply piecing and turning it in a circular motion.'

QUILT SIZE

120 x 120cm when trimmed and bound. All seam allowances are 1cm and are already built into the cutting sizes.

QUILT TOP

You will need approximately 1.5m of fabric A (your plain fabric) and 1.5m of assorted prints. It is important to choose a plain fabric that visually contrasts with your patterned fabrics, so that the overall design is clearly visible.

I used a fine organic ivory cotton calico as my plain cloth and paired it with a variety of Japanese kimono silks in a lovely array of blues. The central square in each block is a vintage silk in ivory and pink. I really like the tactile and visual contrast of smooth silk next to woven cotton, and blue and ivory are a classic combination. It is, in fact, very hard for me NOT to put blue in a quilt.

QUILT BACKING

You will need approximately 1.5m of cloth. The finished size should be 140 x 140cm, so you can use fabric leftovers or a single drop of wide fabric to make the backing.

I kept the quilt simple by using more of the calico on the back.

BINDING

You will need approximately 0.25m of fabric. You can use scraps from the quilt top if you have any left over, or use the binding as an opportunity to introduce a new fabric.

Again, I used the calico so that the design of the quilt stands out.

OTHER MATERIALS

WADDING of your choice, 140 x 140cm.
SEWING THREAD 100 per cent cotton all-purpose thread is best, in a neutral colour.
QUILTING THREAD 100 per cent cotton quilting thread in a colour of your choice.

CUT YOUR FABRIC

Cutting this quilt is very easy. Apart from the 16 centre squares, you simply cut long strips of the same width. See the diagram and photograph on pages 134–5 to plan and cut your fabrics. For fabric C, decide whether you want to freestyle or preplan which fabric goes where. If you want to preplan, trace the diagram and mark in your choices.

SEW YOUR QUILT TOP

Using the diagram on page 134 as your guide, sew each block from the centre piece (1) out. Start by sewing piece 1 to piece 2. Finger-press, turn and sew piece 3 to 1/2. Continue sewing and pressing until you have sewn all 21 pieces together. Take care to keep all the plain fabrics in the correct order – just take your time and refer to the diagram and photograph for guidance. Press the finished block and trim any loose threads.

Repeat to make the remaining 15 Log Cabin blocks.

Lay your 16 blocks out in four rows of four, following the diagram and photograph. If you have freestyled your patterned fabric, you may want to move squares around to create a composition that works.

Make up each row by pinning and sewing the first four blocks together, making sure your seam allowance is consistent. Repeat for the remaining three rows. Press the seams and trim the threads. Pin the first two rows together, ensuring the seams are perfectly aligned. Sew and press. Repeat for the remaining two rows. One last press and thread check, and your quilt top is complete.

SEW YOUR QUILT BACKING

Your quilt backing needs to be a minimum of 140 x 140cm. Join your choice of fabric together until you have a backing the right size. Press all the seams and trim away any excess threads. Your quilt backing is finished.

BUILD YOUR QUILT

Put your quilt sandwich together in your preferred way (see page 182). After you have marked any necessary quilting lines, machine- or hand-quilt using your favourite technique (see page 184). Trim the backing and wadding so that the edges are even and your quilt is square. Finally, make and attach your binding (see page 186).

MAKE IT YOURS

For a queen-size bed, increase the number of blocks to 49 (seven rows of seven). You will need a minimum of 6m of fabric. You can use a variety of cloth or just two fabrics to create graphic diagonal lines. The design can be very pretty or very masculine. As there are many small pieces, it is the perfect quilt in which to use precious scraps or children's clothes.

POJAGI

'GOOD FORTUNE can be captured inside a Pojagi,' according to an ancient Korean saying. This delicately pieced cloth could bring better health, greater respect and happiness for the recipient – a moving notion, don't you think?

Pojagi are most definitely functional cloths. They are used to wrap, carry and cover everything from food to gifts, but they also convey highly symbolic meanings. They serve as an expression of respect - for both the items they wrap and the recipient of the gift. Their value comes from not just the superb stitches, but also their embodiment of an important Korean folk belief: that every pattern within a Pojagi symbolizes the pursuit of happiness and good fortune.

Throughout the Choson dynasty (1392–1910), Korean women lived within an extremely rigid society. Denied any formal education, they embraced practical artistic pursuits as a way of communicating their intelligence and personality. The women took scraps of silk gauze left over from making clothes and used them to make Pojagi wrapping cloths and covers. The fragments were sewn together with a very personal take on pattern and colour, to create something both beautiful and utilitarian. Every traditional Pojagi was prized as a clear expression of the anonymous woman who made it.

All classes in Korean society used Pojagi within strict guidelines of fabric types and use. Inside the Royal Palace, every new item of clothing came wrapped in its own Pojagi. Within all classes, family heirlooms and precious possessions were wrapped in them, and gifts were always presented inside a Pojagi cloth. To this day, the Korean parliament uses them to present important documents and they are also still used to carry things – the original reusable shopping bag, perhaps.

Chogak po (patchwork) is a type of Pojagi made using both old and new cloth, as well as heavier fabrics such as ramie, hemp and silk. Pieced only by commoners, *Chogak po* is no less beautiful for the simpler cloth used. As much as I love the stained-glass effect of a silk Pojagi cloth, I thought a *Chogak po* version would be a wonderful way to turn a subtle group of fabrics into something useful as well as beautiful – thus a quilt instead of a hanging.

So this is my humble homage to the delights of Pojagi. Like the *Chogak po* version, my quilt uses a mixture of fabrics. Although my design has a preplanned layout, it offers an opportunity to mix different types of fabric as well as old and new.

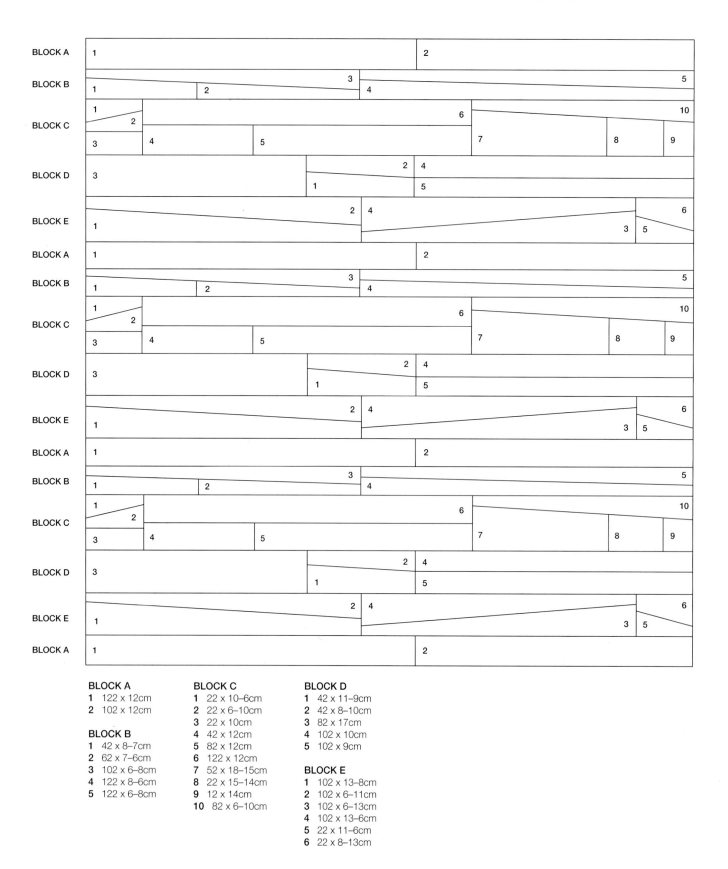

BLOCK A
1 122 x 12cm
2 102 x 12cm

BLOCK B
1 42 x 8–7cm
2 62 x 7–6cm
3 102 x 6–8cm
4 122 x 8–6cm
5 122 x 6–8cm

BLOCK C
1 22 x 10–6cm
2 22 x 6–10cm
3 22 x 10cm
4 42 x 12cm
5 82 x 12cm
6 122 x 12cm
7 52 x 18–15cm
8 22 x 15–14cm
9 12 x 14cm
10 82 x 6–10cm

BLOCK D
1 42 x 11–9cm
2 42 x 8–10cm
3 82 x 17cm
4 102 x 10cm
5 102 x 9cm

BLOCK E
1 102 x 13–8cm
2 102 x 6–11cm
3 102 x 6–13cm
4 102 x 13–6cm
5 22 x 11–6cm
6 22 x 8–13cm

'It was believed that every
pattern within a Pojagi
symbolized the pursuit of
happiness and good fortune.'

QUILT SIZE
220 x 220cm when trimmed and bound. All seam allowances are 1cm and are included in the cutting sizes.

QUILT TOP
You will need approximately 6–7m of fabric. The cut pieces vary in length from 12cm to 122cm, so make sure you have some large pieces of cloth to draw from.

My quilt colour palette started from two pieces of kimono silk – abstractly patterned in wonderfully subtle shades of blue, green, taupe and mauve. I used this as the base for selecting six different plain cottons. I bought 1.25m of each and used any leftovers for the backing, binding and other quilts in the collection.

QUILT BACKING
You will need approximately 6m of fabric. The finished size should be at least 240 x 240cm. You can use fabric leftovers as well as fabric from a bolt of cloth to make the backing.

I very happily (and maybe slightly extravagantly) used a vintage silk sari that had a lovely sandwashed feel, ensuring tactile luxury to sleep under. The sari wasn't quite large enough, so I pieced some cotton fabrics together and joined them to it to make a backing the size I needed.

BINDING
You will need approximately 0.5m of fabric. You can use scraps from the quilt top if you have any left over, or use the binding as an opportunity to introduce a new fabric.

I used leftover fabric from the quilt top for my binding, just cutting and piecing strips randomly from the plain cottons.

OTHER MATERIALS
WADDING of your choice, 240 x 240cm.
SEWING THREAD 100 per cent cotton all-purpose thread is best, in a neutral colour.
QUILTING THREAD 100 per cent cotton quilting thread in a colour of your choice.

CUT YOUR FABRIC

The Pojagi quilt is similar to the Boro quilt (see page 100), in that it is made from repeating blocks and requires you to cut fabric at an angle. I am sure the diagram on page 140 looks a little intimidating. I promise you it isn't – just break the quilt down into manageable sections and set aside a morning or an afternoon to get into the swing of it.

The quilt is made from five repeating blocks (A–E). Each block is made up of a number of pieces that need to be cut and sewn together in a logical order to form the completed block – simple. Block A is cut and pieced four times; blocks B, C, D and E are cut and pieced three times.

If you have small pieces of cloth or pieces of a certain size, plan those into your quilt first. Mark them on the diagram or trace the diagram with tracing paper first and mark them on the copy. Cut the pieces out, mark the number on the back of the fabric with pencil or tailor's chalk and set them aside.

If you are using a limited number of fabrics, as I have, it is best to plan everything on the diagram before you start cutting. This is so you can avoid joining two pieces of the same fabric together. Just mark each fabric on the diagram, or you can colour it in using coloured pencils or watercolours to get an idea of how it will look before you start. If you have lots of different fabrics, then you don't need to plan the composition so rigidly.

Lay your fabrics out in individual piles near your cutting mat, so that you can easily see the choices you have to work with. Then clear a good-sized space close to your cutting and sewing area, where you can lay out your pieces in order as you cut them to see the block forming.

Start with the first block B and use the diagram as your guide. Cut all five pieces in the order they are numbered and lay them next to each other to see the block forming. If you have preplanned your fabrics, this is an opportunity to change things. If you are choosing as you go, make sure you utilize any patterns or stripes to create a lovely 'movement' in your quilt. For the pieces with angled edges, first cut the fixed measurement and then mark in the two angled measurements before you cut them.

Mark the number on the back of each piece using a pencil or tailor's chalk, in case you have to stop making before you have finished piecing a block.

When you have finished cutting your first block B, you need to sew it together before moving on to a new block.

SEW YOUR QUILT TOP

Starting with block B and following the diagram, sew each piece together in the order that you have cut it. Sew B1 to B2 and press the seam. Then sew B3 to this block and press the seam. Sew B4 to B5 and press the seam. Then sew this to the first block. Press the seam and trim away any excess thread. Your first block B is complete.

Cut and sew your remaining two block Bs. Then move on to the remaining blocks, leaving block A until last.

Lay all 16 blocks out, following the order of the diagram. If you haven't preplanned your fabric placements, you can move each of the blocks around to get a composition you like. Photograph the options so that you can compare layouts and choose the one you like most.

Pin and sew each block together until you have joined all 16. It is important to use pins at this stage, to prevent the seams from twisting and stretching.

Press all the seams and trim away any excess sewing thread. Your quilt top is finished.

SEW YOUR QUILT BACKING

Your quilt backing needs to be a minimum of 240 x 240cm. Simply join together your choice of fabric until you have a backing the right size – this is a great way of practising freestyling. Press all the seams, trim away any excess threads and your quilt backing is complete.

BUILD YOUR QUILT

Put your quilt sandwich together in your preferred way (see page 182). After you have marked any necessary quilting lines, machine- or hand-quilt using your favourite technique (see page 184). Trim the backing and wadding so that the edges are even and your quilt is square. Finally, make and attach your binding (see page 186).

MAKE IT YOURS

You can create a true Pojagi by piecing the quilt top using only sheer fabrics, such as silk or cotton organdie. You could create an exquisite curtain panel or a very special throw from this, or piece smaller sections for a stunning set of cushion covers. You can simplify the number of blocks used down to three – B, D and E work well together – and you can, of course, adjust the quilt size by the number of blocks that you use.

IRISH CHAIN

IT IS IRISH in name, but probably American in design. Like many other quilts, its true history is doubtless a mixture of folklore and fact.

Patchwork quilts were made in Ireland from the eighteenth century. The wives of the English landed gentry taught their servants many needlework skills, including patchwork and quilting. The servants passed on their new skills and passion to their families, neighbours and others in their close communities. Quilt-making thrived and became an Irish tradition. The early patterns reflected English quilt designs, including English Piecing, Crazy, Strip and Frame quilts. Quilt designs did not develop until Irish people started to emigrate, as they lived in small, isolated communities with little, if any, disposable income.

Traditionally, Irish patchwork was made from a top and backing, stitched together with simple patterns. Quilts were purely functional and constructed with this in mind. Women used old wool and hand-woven fabrics, as well as remnants or worn-out clothes. As is the case with many of the quilts made from necessity, the majority of these early quilts no longer exist – either because they were worn out and reused, or because they were destroyed. People often raze reminders of poverty, and, as much as we would love to see these original quilts, it is understandable that the community wanted to look forwards, not backwards.

Irish quilts soon developed a very strong American influence in both their pattern and style. The Irish Chain pattern was known in America from the early nineteenth century, but it is possible that it was originally made in Ireland. There have long been close ties between the two countries, so it isn't too hard to imagine the Irish Chain design being developed between the new immigrants and their families left in Ireland. Many immigrants carried their belongings wrapped in a quilt, and others made them on the long journey. Quilts were often sent to America as wedding presents or gifts for the young settlers. These quilts became important, as they were a tangible link between those who had started a new life and the families they had left behind.

I wanted this quilt to be the very simplest version it could be, so I created a design based on a single Irish Chain pattern. I have seen many versions of this quilt, but have always been drawn to the sparseness of this style. I think that it is both traditional and relevant for how we live now.

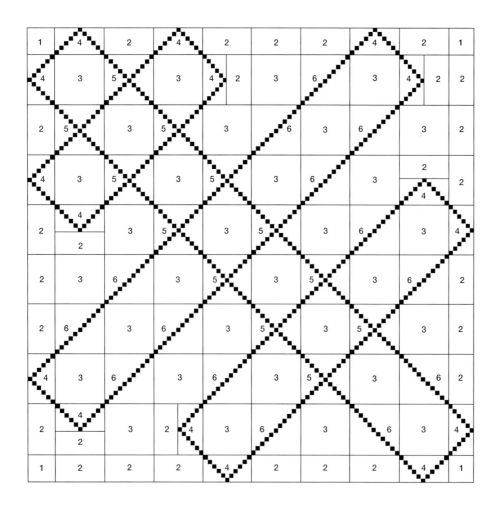

Pieced Blocks 4–6
These are made by piecing together 4cm-wide strips cut from prep blocks A–K.

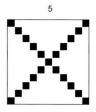

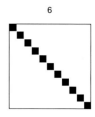

Prep Blocks A–K
These are cut into 4cm-wide strips, which are pieced together to create blocks 4–6.

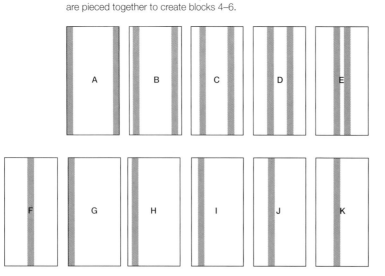

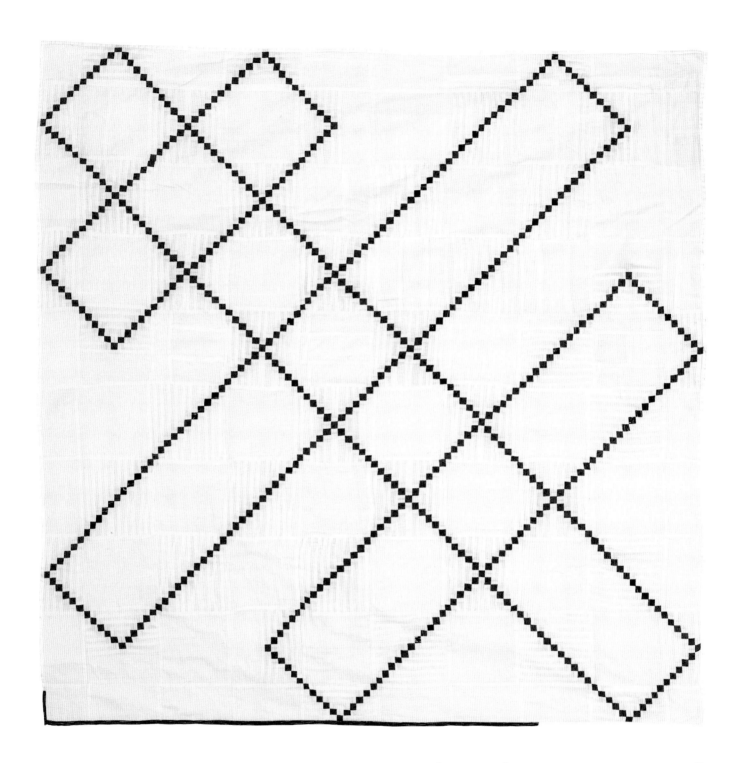

'I love the sparseness of this style of quilt – its simple design is based on a single Irish Chain pattern.'

QUILT SIZE
200 x 200cm when trimmed and bound. All seam allowances are 1cm and are already built into the cutting sizes.

QUILT TOP
You will need approximately 6m of your base fabric (A) and approximately 1m for your small squares (B). You can use one fabric for your squares or an assortment in similar colours or patterns. Your base cloth should be a medium-weight cotton, as you need to cut and re-sew a lot of strips together.

I wanted this quilt to feel 'airy', so I used my favourite khadi cotton in ivory as my base cloth, and antique Japanese silk for my tiny squares. The majority of the squares were cut from one fabric, but I also used scraps of complementary silk to add interest. You will be handling this quilt a great deal as you piece it, so make sure the fabric you choose is robust and easy to sew.

QUILT BACKING
You will need approximately 5m of fabric. The finished size should be at least 220 x 220cm, so you can use fabric leftovers, a sheet or any other robust cotton, as well as fabric from a bolt of cloth to make the backing.

I used a soft green cotton for contrast and simplicity.

BINDING
You will need approximately 0.5m of fabric. You can use scraps from the quilt top if you have any left over, or use the binding as an opportunity to introduce a new fabric.

I completed the quilt with ivory cotton binding, so that the focus was on the design itself, not the edges.

OTHER MATERIALS
WADDING of your choice, 220 x 220cm.
SEWING THREAD 100 per cent cotton all-purpose thread is best, in a neutral colour.
QUILTING THREAD 100 per cent cotton quilting thread in a colour of your choice.

CUT AND SEW YOUR FABRIC
The Irish Chain is easy to piece but requires patience and precision. There is a great deal of cutting and piecing, so set aside chunks of time to cut and piece sections. Use envelopes to store each of the different block sizes once you have cut them and focus on just one part at a time. The quilt is made from three plain blocks (1–3) and three pieced blocks (4–6) – look at the diagram and photograph on pages 146–7 to see how the design works. I found it easiest to cut all the blocks and strips together, but then pieced and re-cut block by block.

For your plain blocks, cut the following from fabric A:
Block 1: 4 of 14 x 14cm
Block 2: 28 of 14 x 22cm
Block 3: 32 of 22 x 22cm

For your small squares, cut 25 4cm-wide strips from fabric B across the width of your fabric. Piece them together to make one long strip. Now concentrate! You will cut and piece 11 different prep blocks (A–K), which you will then re-cut into smaller segments to create the finished blocks. Look at the diagrams on page 146 to see how these look. Cut the following:
A: Fabric A, 1 of 20 x 160cm; fabric B, 2 of 4 x 160cm
B: Fabric A, 1 of 16 x 160cm, 2 of 4 x 160cm; fabric B, 2 of 4 x 160cm

C: Fabric A, 1 of 12 x 160cm, 2 of 6 x 160cm; fabric B, 2 of 4 x 160cm
D: Fabric A, 3 of 8 x 160cm; fabric B, 2 of 4 x 160cm
E: Fabric A, 1 of 4 x 160cm, 2 of 10 x 160cm; fabric B, 2 of 4 x 160cm
F: Fabric A, 2 of 12 x 168cm; fabric B, 1 of 4 x 168cm
G: Fabric A, 1 of 22 x 112cm; fabric B, 1 of 4 x 112cm
H: Fabric A, 1 of 4 x 112cm, 1 of 20 x 112cm; fabric B, 1 of 4 x 112cm
I: Fabric A, 1 of 6 x 112cm, 1 of 18 x 112cm; fabric B, 1 of 4 x 112cm
J: Fabric A, 1 of 8 x 112cm, 1 of 16 x 112cm; fabric B, 1 of 4 x 112cm
K: Fabric A, 1 of 10 x 112cm, 1 of 14 x 112cm; fabric B, 1 of 4 x 112cm

Starting with prep block A, sew the pieces together in the order of the diagram. Press the seams. Then cut the block across its width into 4cm-wide segments. Put aside. Repeat these steps for the remaining prep blocks.

SEW YOUR QUILT TOP
There are three different pieced blocks that you need to sew together before you can piece the quilt top. It is important to be accurate with your sewing in this step so that all the blocks line up. Look at the diagrams of blocks

4, 5 and 6. You will see how each of the blocks consists of segments from the prep blocks A–K. Once you have created your first pieced block, it should all make sense.

Start with block 4 and piece the relevant strips together by following the diagram – A, B, C, D, E, F. Make 16 of block 4, press all the seams and set aside.

For block 5, piece together A, B, C, D, E, F, E, D, C, B, A. Make 12 of block 5, press all the seams and set aside.

For block 6, piece together G, H, I, J, K, F, K, J, I, H, G, flipping the direction of the strips after F to create the diagonal. Make 14 of block 6, press the seams and set aside.

To piece your quilt top together, lay your blocks out in the order of the main diagram on page 146.

Pin and sew all the blocks in the first row together, being consistent with your seam allowance. Repeat for the remaining nine rows and press all the seams.

Pin the top two rows together, being careful to match the seamlines precisely. Sew them together, checking that your stitching is accurate before you move on. Continue pinning and sewing until you have pieced all ten rows. Press the seams and remove any loose threads.

SEW YOUR QUILT BACKING
Your quilt backing needs to be a minimum of 220 x 220cm. Join your choice of fabric together until you have a backing the right size. Press all the seams and trim away any excess threads. Your quilt backing is now complete.

BUILD YOUR QUILT
Put your quilt sandwich together in your preferred way (see page 182). After you have marked any necessary quilting lines, machine- or hand-quilt using your favourite technique (see page 184). Trim the backing and wadding so that the edges are even and your quilt is square. Finally, make and attach your binding (see page 186).

MAKE IT YOURS
If you would like a more traditional Irish Chain design, you can trace the pattern and 'fill in' the missing blocks. It is then easy to change the number of plain and pieced blocks you will need. Of course, you could do the reverse and simplify the chain even further. The small squares don't have to be one colour – you could use a different fabric for each piece, if you have the patience.

RALLI

A RALLI QUILT is the perfect storyteller. It narrates the lives of women and their families, communities, cultures and traditions. Each quilt is a tribute to the individual maker's creativity and their family history. A colour may indicate where her community is based, while a certain piece of antique cloth may reveal her living conditions and place in society.

Ralli quilts are made in the southern states of Pakistan - Sindh, Balochistan and in the Cholistan Desert – as well as in Gujarat and Rajasthan. The name comes from the local word *ralanna*, which means to mix or connect – a wonderful sentiment for cloth. The creation of Ralli is important in every sector of society, as they are made by Hindu and Muslim women of different castes, rural villages, nomadic tribes and established towns. It is very rare for a Ralli quilt to be bought or sold. They are made by women for their family to sleep under, sit on or carry. For a very humble and utilitarian object, a Ralli quilt is still a measure of wealth in some areas and is an integral part of a girl's dowry.

The quilts are made from scraps of cotton fabric hand-dyed to the maker's colour palette. Much of the cloth used is old shalwar kameez (a traditional dress), tie-dye, ajrak (block-printed shawls) or other shawl fabric, everything adding to the history and story of the maker and her life. Several layers of fabric are used to make up the quilt, with mostly new cloth for the decorative top layer and recycled fabric for the inner layers and backing.

The quilt top is designed and pieced by one woman. She carefully forms patterns and symbols from cloth, some simple and some complex, relying on her own memories and those of her mother to create her unique design. Every maker adjusts patterns and colour palettes to create an individual point of view.

The quilt is then stitched together by the maker's family and extended community of women. As a quilt is usually stitched together in one day, the process is an important time for talking, sharing and singing. The quilt layers are placed on reed mats and quickly tacked together. The women sit on the ground at opposite ends of the quilt and sew all the layers together, using thick coloured thread stitched in straight, parallel lines. No patterns, frames or tools are used – just their 'eye' and a needle and thread.

A Ralli quilt encapsulates my love for the craft of quilting. It is pure creativity, anthropology and love, enmeshed in cloth and thread. My version is based on a classic design that I have seen hundreds of times. While every one of these Ralli quilts has roughly the same layout, no two are alike physically or spiritually – and I like that.

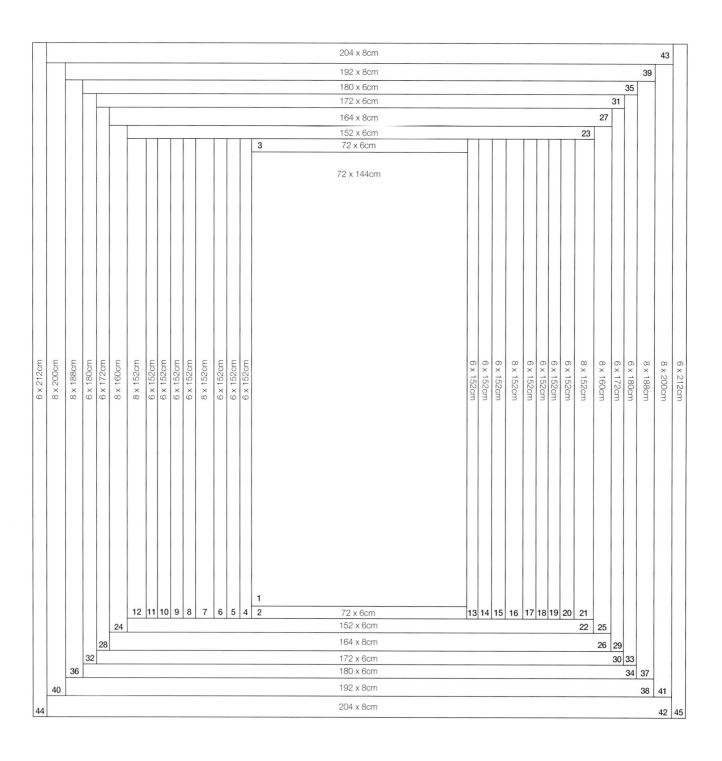

204 x 8cm — 43
192 x 8cm — 39
180 x 6cm — 35
172 x 6cm — 31
164 x 8cm — 27
152 x 6cm — 23
3 — 72 x 6cm

72 x 144cm

6 x 212cm
8 x 200cm
8 x 188cm
6 x 180cm
6 x 172cm
8 x 160cm
8 x 152cm
9 x 152cm
6 x 152cm
6 x 152cm
6 x 152cm
8 x 152cm
6 x 152cm
6 x 152cm
6 x 152cm

6 x 152cm
6 x 152cm
6 x 152cm
8 x 152cm
6 x 152cm
6 x 152cm
6 x 152cm
6 x 152cm
8 x 152cm
8 x 160cm
6 x 172cm
6 x 180cm
8 x 188cm
8 x 200cm
6 x 212cm

1
12 11 10 9 8 7 6 5 4 2 — 72 x 6cm — 13 14 15 16 17 18 19 20 21
24 — 152 x 6cm — 22 25
28 — 164 x 8cm — 26 29
32 — 172 x 6cm — 30 33
36 — 180 x 6cm — 34 37
40 — 192 x 8cm — 38 41
44 — 204 x 8cm — 42 45

'The Ralli is a very simple quilt to cut and sew but it looks incredibly dramatic when completed.'

QUILT SIZE

210 x 210cm when trimmed and bound. All seam allowances are 1cm and are already built into the cutting sizes.

QUILT TOP

You will need approximately 6m of fabric. There is very little wastage from this quilt, as you are cutting continuous strips. Your central piece needs to be 72 x 144cm. All the other pieces in the quilt design are narrow strips that can be sewn together to create the required length.

I used a mixture of vintage silk saris, starting with the stunning blue and woven metallic cloth as my central piece. I then selected other saris that picked up different colours and tones from it. See Fabric and Other Materials, page 169.

QUILT BACKING

You will need approximately 5.5–6m of fabric. The finished size should be at least 230 x 230cm, so you can use left-over sari silk as well as any fabric from a bolt of cloth to make the backing.

BINDING

You will need approximately 0.5m of fabric. You can use scraps from the quilt top if you have any left over, or use the binding as an opportunity to introduce a new fabric.

I used the scraps from the quilt top so that the binding blended seamlessly into the quilt design.

OTHER MATERIALS

WADDING of your choice, 230 x 230cm.
SEWING THREAD 100 per cent cotton all-purpose thread is best, in a neutral colour.
QUILTING THREAD 100 per cent cotton quilting thread in a colour of your choice.

CUT YOUR FABRIC

Choose and cut your central piece and set it aside. You can then either preplan the placement of the other fabrics or choose which to use in which strip as you work.

For the strips, you have two possible methods. You can either cut each strip to the measurements marked on the diagram on page 152, or cut and join continuous strips at two widths – you will need at least 41m of 6cm-wide fabric and at least 29m of 8cm-wide fabric. If you have preplanned where each fabric will go, choose the first option. If you are happy to freestyle, you can do either. Cutting exact lengths will make it easier to be precise, but one continuous strip will be faster – what choices! You can cut this entire quilt in a morning or an afternoon.

SEW YOUR QUILT TOP

To ensure super-straight seams when sewing long strips together, simply rotate your work 180° each time – sew the first seam top to bottom and the next seam bottom to top. Although I am not obsessed with perfectly straight quilts, I think this design benefits from being precise.

Follow the diagram on page 152 to ensure that you sew the strips together in the right order. I often place a cross or tick on the pattern as I go, as interruptions make it very easy to lose your place.

Start by sewing your centre piece, 1, to strip 2. Then add strip 3 and press the seams. Continue to piece the quilt together using your chosen method – either exact lengths or continuous. If you use the latter method, take care not to stretch the seams as you sew and trim off the continuous strip to start at the next seam. When you have sewn strip 21, press all the seams and trim any threads.

Continue sewing one strip at a time, following the order of the diagram and pressing after every two seams. Once you have sewn the last strip, 45, trim any loose threads.

SEW YOUR QUILT BACKING

Your quilt backing needs to be a minimum of 230 x 230cm. Piece your chosen fabrics together, press all the seams (front and back) and trim away any excess threads.

BUILD YOUR QUILT

Put your quilt sandwich together in your preferred way (see page 182). Mark any necessary quilting lines and machine- or hand-quilt (see page 184). Trim the backing and wadding so the edges are even and your quilt is square. Finally, make and attach your binding (see page 186).

MAKE IT YOURS

This is the perfect quilt for using a spectacular fabric at the centre. Take time to hunt out something special and find the right supporting fabrics. Reduce or increase the size of the quilt by simply adding or subtracting strips.

ALBUM

THIS IS IT – the very last quilt, a tangible culmination of every quilt design and their makers.

Sampler quilts have been around since the 1840s and were used to record the fashionable quilt designs of the day. As the popularity of Frame quilts gave way to the new block style, a Sampler quilt gave the maker an opportunity to try every design that took her fancy. They were individually made or pieced as a collaborative effort, sometimes by friends and family members who lived apart. They were also used as study documents for young women, in the same way as needlework samplers. Using the Sampler as a touchstone, a quilt maker could choose a pattern or patterns that she liked the most to develop into another quilt.

Sampler quilts developed at the same time as Album and Friendship quilts, with all three often overlapping. They all used the same concept of many different blocks, but whereas a Sampler quilt was probably for personal and teaching use, the other two had greater emotional meaning and purpose. Album quilts were communal projects made to commemorate special events and to raise funds for key causes. They were an opportunity to show the maker's political point of view, as well as to express friendship between each of the makers. Individuals designed and contributed their own blocks and these were beautifully made.

Friendship quilts are possibly the most emotive, as they were made as a keepsake for one person. Each maker would create their own block, which they often signed and inscribed with a message. Sometimes such quilts were made for someone important within the community, but they are generally revered as quilts for people emigrating to the New World. It was unlikely that these people would ever return home, so this quilt was a deeply treasured reminder of the loved ones and places they had left behind.

This quilt design underlines why I will always make quilts. A quilt is an extraordinary gift, as it represents your precious time as well as your thoughts and emotions. My Album/Sampler/Friendship quilt has a small block from most of the quilts in this book. Each block is a reminder of the people who originally made these designs, as well as the lives they lived, and I am truly humbled by them all.

SEMINOLE

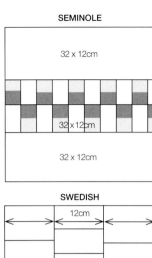

32 x 12cm

32 x 12cm

32 x 12cm

IRISH CHAIN

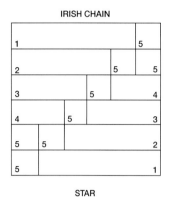

WELSH BARS

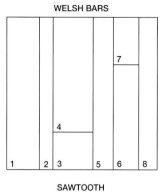

RALLI

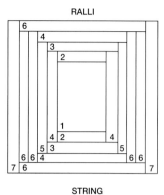

SWEDISH

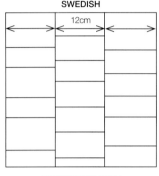

12cm

STAR

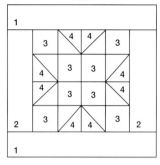

SAWTOOTH

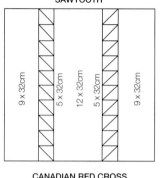

9 x 32cm   5 x 32cm   12 x 32cm   5 x 32cm   9 x 32cm

STRING

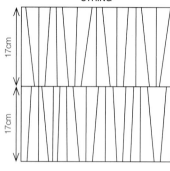

17cm

17cm

DRUNKARD'S PATH

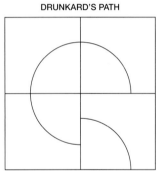

STRIPPY

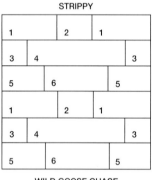

CANADIAN RED CROSS

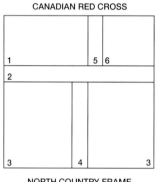

RAIL FENCE

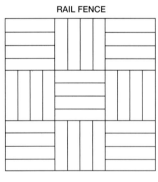

WILD GOOSE CHASE

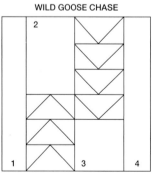

NORTH COUNTRY FRAME

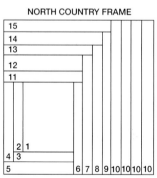

**WILD GOOSE
CHASE**
1 7 x 32cm
2 12 x 17cm
3 12 x 12cm
4 7 x 32cm
The two geese
blocks need to
be 12 x 17cm
and 12 x 22cm.

**NORTH
COUNTRY
FRAME**
1 12 x 16cm
2 4 x 16cm
3 14 x 4cm
4 4 x 18cm
5 16 x 4cm
6 4 x 20cm
7 4 x 25cm
8 4 x 27cm
9 4 x 30cm

10 4 x 32cm
11 18 x 4cm
12 18 x 5cm
13 20 x 4cm
14 22 x 5cm
15 24 x 4cm

**LOG CABIN
ENGLISH PIECING
POSTAGE STAMP**
For the above
designs, replicate
a block from the
main pattern.

**KANTHA
WHOLECLOTH
GEE'S BEND**
For the above
designs, freestyle
a block measuring
32 x 32cm.

IRISH CHAIN
1 27 x 7cm
2 22 x 7cm
3 17 x 7cm
4 12 x 7cm
5 7 x 7cm

WELSH BARS
1 8 x 32cm
2 5 x 32cm
3 10 x 9cm
4 10 x 25cm
5 6 x 32cm

6 8 x 23cm
7 8 x 11cm
8 5 x 32cm

RALLI
1 12 x 16cm
2 12 x 4cm
3 16 x 4cm
4 20 x 4cm
5 4 x 24cm
6 4 x 28cm
7 4 x 32cm

SWEDISH
Create three
randomly pieced
strips measuring
12 x 32cm,
then sew them
together to create
your block.

STAR
1 32 x 7cm
2 7 x 22cm
3 7 x 7cm

4 9 x 9cm,
cut across the
diagonal to
create triangles.

**DRUNKARD'S
PATH**
Download
the pattern
from www.
cassandraellis.
co.uk/
worldofquilts.

STRIPPY
1 13.5 x 7cm
2 9 x 7cm
3 6.5 x 7cm
4 23 x 7cm
5 10.5 x 7cm
6 15 x 7cm

**CANADIAN
RED CROSS**
1 19 x 12cm
2 32 x 5cm
3 15.5 x 19cm

4 5 x 19cm
5 5 x 12cm
6 12 x 12cm

RAIL FENCE
Make up 9 mini
blocks of four
strips, each
measuring 4.5 x
12cm; the mini
blocks are 12 x
12cm before being
stitched together.

QUILT SIZE

120 x 150cm when trimmed and bound – but it can be increased or reduced in increments of 30cm. All seam allowances are 1cm and are already built into the cutting sizes.

QUILT TOP

For my very last quilt I decided to use only neutrals – all the white, cream, linen, tea and ivory fabrics that I had used throughout the other quilts in the book. I wanted the colour palette to take a back seat so that the designs really were king. Being the final quilt I made out of the 25, it truly is a summary of all the research, cutting, piecing and stitching I have done during the past 12 months.

For a quilt of this size you will need approximately 4m of fabric, depending on which blocks you use.

This can be a bundle of remnants because most pieces are small, or you can use a selection of 0.5m pieces and fat quarters.

I grabbed all the light-coloured fabric I had left and crossed my fingers that there was enough.

QUILT BACKING

You will need approximately 2m of fabric. The finished size should be at least 140 x 170cm, so you can use fabric leftovers, a sheet or any other robust cotton, as well as fabric from a bolt of cloth to make the backing. I suggest for this quilt that you use something special.

I used a combination of silk saris and the dusky pink khadi cotton left over from the Drunkard's Path quilt. I was so thrilled with that colour that I wanted to use it on my last – but very special – quilt.

BINDING

You will need approximately 0.5m of fabric. You can use scraps from the quilt top if you have any left over, or use the binding as an opportunity to introduce a new fabric.

I kept it plain and pale by using an ivory cotton voile.

OTHER MATERIALS

WADDING of your choice, 140 x 170cm.
SEWING THREAD 100 per cent cotton all-purpose thread is best, in a neutral colour.
QUILTING THREAD 100 per cent cotton quilting thread in a colour of your choice.

CUT YOUR FABRIC

Before you cut any fabric, look at the individual diagrams on page 160 and the photograph on page 161. Each of the 20 blocks used to make this quilt is a miniature version of a quilt in this book. Choose the one, five or 20 patterns that you want to use for your version of an Album quilt, then cut the fabrics according to the diagram. Refer back to the corresponding quilt design if you need to be reminded of the technique.

Every block is made from small pieces, so any mistakes can be easily rectified. Once you have cut a complete block, label the pieces and place them in an envelope to avoid confusion. Once you have cut all 20 blocks, you are ready to sew – or you can cut and sew block by block. Each block should take no more than two hours, so this is a great way to create something beautiful in a short space of time.

SEW YOUR QUILT TOP

Lay your first block out in the order that you will piece it together. Refer to the instructions on the corresponding quilt and piece it together using the same method. For example, the Log Cabin block is an exact replica of the larger quilt, while the North Country Frame block is a miniature adaptation of its larger version. Although each block is scaled down, the principles are the same. Press all seams and trim loose threads as you go. Once you have made all 20 blocks, you are ready to piece them together.

Clear a space and lay your blocks out in five rows of four blocks. Move and spin the blocks around until you find a composition that you love. Remember to record the options with your phone, tablet or camera so that you can choose the layout you like the most.

Starting with the top row, join each row together by pinning and sewing the four blocks together, making sure your seam allowance is consistent. Repeat for the remaining four rows. Press the seams and trim any loose threads. Pin the first two rows together, ensuring that you have lined up the seams perfectly. Sew and press. Repeat for the remaining three rows. One last press and thread check, and your quilt top is complete.

SEW YOUR QUILT BACKING

Your quilt backing needs to be a minimum of 140 x 170cm. Use the excess fabric from your quilt top or

introduce something new. Join your choice of fabric together until you have a backing the right size. Press all the seams and trim away any excess threads. Your quilt backing is now complete.

BUILD YOUR QUILT

Put your quilt sandwich together in your preferred way (see page 182). After you have marked any necessary quilting lines, machine- or hand-quilt using your favourite technique (see page 184). Trim the backing and wadding so that the edges are even and your quilt is square. Finally, make and attach your binding (see page 186).

MAKE IT YOURS

What can't you do with this quilt? There are 20 miniature versions to replicate, duplicate or not use at all. You could also experiment with adjusting designs – they are only 30cm square. This quilt can be as large or as small as you like and you can use two fabrics or 200.

'Made up from 20 blocks that are miniature versions of other quilts in the book, the Album quilt is truly special. Choose your favourite block designs and create a quilt to last a lifetime.'

QUILT

MASTERCLASS

ORIGINALLY, MOST QUILTS were simply made with just fabric, a needle and thread. Sometimes they would be cut and pieced by one woman, at other times it was a communal effort – the quilters shared tips and ideas on quilt-making, as well as their hands and time.

The past 50 years have seen the introduction of lots of tools and products – some of which are very useful – and a plethora of definitions, tips and rules on quilting – some of which are not. I think it is very important to remember that essentially a quilt is fabric cut into pieces and sewn back together again. There are many methods and options – you just need to find a combination that suits you.

I hope you will find the following pages useful. I wanted to make quilt-making easier both to understand and to do. There are some great tools available and many techniques that I have learnt over the years, which do ease the process, giving you the freedom to be creative. I advise you to read this section before launching into a project because I think it will explain what a quilt is and help you to plan what you want to make and how you would like to go about it.

Design ideas

Before I plan a new quilt design or theme, I go hunting for inspiration. At this stage I am thinking about colours and moods, shapes and feelings. By pulling together a physical moodboard of what I want the quilt to be and the overall feel I want for it, I start to form the outline of how I want it to be designed and pieced.

Every country and culture has its own quilt palette. I could have replicated these like for like, but then it wouldn't have been a reflection of how I feel about these tribes and their quilts. So I went hunting and gathering, searching for a considered palette and feeling, to tie them all together.

It started with several galleries that I adore and a florist whose work I greatly admire. London's Tate Britain is a revered and much-loved art gallery. In the summer that I started preparing for this book, the curators rehung all of the artworks in a new and dynamic way. It was extraordinary and very exciting. I absorbed J M W Turner's watercolours and swatches, as well as the art of the famous St Ives set. This led me to Kettle's Yard in Cambridge, where much of their work is displayed, to explore them and others further. In turn, this made me think about the optimism and calmness of much of the fine and decorative art from that period. I gathered books and postcards, visited those places again and again, and took many photographs. Then I looked at the work of a New York florist. Her eye for colour and her use of wild plants are incredibly uplifting, which somehow added to the artists' work I had already gathered. Because it was summer, I visited gardens, took photographs of plants and just soaked it all up. I then created a moodboard from everything I had accumulated, and added words and quotes that I felt brought it together. And there it was: my (hopefully) calm, artisanal and optimistic palette. From this overarching theme, I then created a mini design board for every quilt, which helped me with both the design and my fabric choices.

To create your own moodboard, find postcards or pictures of buildings, galleries or gardens, and take photographs of anything that moves you. Tear images from magazines or raid the pile you have already accumulated. Visit ribbon shops and button shops, vintage clothing markets and fabric stores. Watch old films and read books on gardens, fashion and furniture design. Rummage through your snaps of fantastic holidays and buy sample pots of paint, or dabble in watercolour or oil paints. Slowly a theme will emerge.

Organize the elements into a three-dimensional vignette and photograph it. It is the combination of everything that creates the overarching idea. Print it out or keep it on your phone or tablet. You are now ready both to choose your fabric and decide on an actual quilt design. Are you excited?

Fabric and other materials

FABRIC

Start by trusting your instinct. Fabric – especially the fabric you use for quilts – can be a highly controversial subject, which I find slightly peculiar. Everyone has an opinion on what you can and can't use – in terms of type of fabric, colours and patterns, as well as how many fabrics you can use in one quilt. Of course, it is only what you think that matters. You can certainly be a devotee of purpose-made quilting cloth – there are some fabulous collections available. Or you might be a recycling fanatic, who turns every worn-out shirt, dress or sheet into a new creation.

I have taught hundreds of women and men to quilt, and I have yet to see two people who have exactly the same taste in design or choice of cloth. One of the most inspiring aspects of the workshops I run is everyone's honest appreciation and excitement for individual fabric choices and combinations. Quilts take a long time to make – anything from days to years – so I believe the choice of fabric and palette has to be something you are really very happy with.

Hopefully, you will have spent some time putting together your own design ideas. Use this moodboard as your guide for choosing fabrics – either new or from your stash. You can mix old and contemporary fabrics, recycled clothes and new fat quarters.

As much as I appreciate and use quilting cottons, I must admit that I am more inspired by curating my own collection of individual pieces of cloth, because then it is truly 'me'. I will always use silk and cotton together, and will most definitely mix Indian cloth with African, and French with Japanese. This is what holds true for me, but I encourage you to find your own signature combinations and fabric choices.

You can use most types of fabric in a quilt, including those of different weights. However, it is best to piece like to like – for example, fine silk and thick velvet won't hold together well, but silk to cotton to velvet will.

There is a huge choice of cotton cloth available, and for a practical quilt this is best. It is robust, easy to sew and can withstand the rough and tumble of everyday life really well. However, you may have a passion for African wax prints or vintage saris, so feel free to use them. You might have a vast collection of your husband's (old) business shirts or some of your children's best dresses to use, which, of course, you can. There are many extraordinary antique quilts that are made from nothing more than scraps – whether of clothes, bed covers, sugar sacks or old curtains – and they are usually breathtakingly beautiful.

You can use vintage or antique fabrics in a quilt, but be aware that they will age faster than any new cotton. You can always patch or repair these pieces – like the original Boro quilts (see page 100) – to add another chapter to your quilt's story.

Silk can be fragile and it will fade in sunlight. Very old silk may rip or disintegrate when you quilt it, so you might just use it in small pieces to preserve it, or use it for the backing. Very fine fabric, including lace, can be strengthened by backing it with a second piece of fabric or cotton interfacing. Interfacing should be ironed onto the back of knit fabrics, as it makes the stretchy fabric behave like a woven cloth.

I love silk, but I never use it in quilts for small children or teenagers because it simply isn't practical. Think about your quilt's intended home before you choose which fabrics you are going to use.

Last but not least, I don't think man-made fabrics, such as polyester, work well in a quilt. They behave differently from natural-fibre fabrics when they are washed and sewn – plus, they don't feel great against your skin.

If you are buying new cloth from a bolt, I would recommend that you purchase at least half a metre. Fat quarters are useful for only a certain type of quilt, so it is better to have flexibility, especially if you don't know your finished design. If there is fabric left over, you can always use it to piece the backing or binding – or use it for another project.

Any scarves, scraps or dresses come as they are and you will need to work around their limitations. Remove any collars, cuffs and waistbands from clothing, then cut through the side seams and underarm seams to maximize the usable fabric.

Curating your fabric choices into a quilt can be a bit mind-boggling. You will have your own instinctive palette and feel, and you need to trust that. We all choose how we dress and decorate our homes, so plan your quilt in the same way. It may not be what anyone else likes but that isn't important. Pull together your design ideas and gather up your selection of fabrics. Choose colour combinations by adding and subtracting fabrics to and from your pile. Take your time, as this is an incredibly important part of making your quilt. Different colours and patterns will definitely change its overall look and mood.

The scale of patterns is also important. I work on the principle that there are three levels of scale: first are the large or dominant patterns – such as an enormous rose print or detailed embroidery; then there are medium patterns – a toile or leafy print, for example; last are the nonpatterns – these can be plain, textured or with a small repeat print, such as checks or spots. There are many 'rules' stipulating the proportion of small-, medium- and large-scale patterns that it is optimum to use within a quilt design. My view is that if you are going to use a big pattern in your quilt, you need to include patterns that fall within the other two scales to give it both prominence and breathing space. Otherwise, no rules are necessary. Look at the quilts in the book to see how patterns can work together.

PREPARING FABRICS
To wash or not to wash before cutting? I am afraid the answer isn't a simple yes or no. Fabrics are not created equal when it comes to treatment, dye-run and shrinkage, so it is best to treat each fabric individually when you choose to prewash or not.

Commercial quilting cotton doesn't need to be prewashed. It will have very little shrinkage and no dye-run, but you can wash it if you prefer a softer finish. Some commercially produced fabric has a gelatine-like size on it, which makes the fabric look shiny and feel firm to the touch. This will disappear when you wash the fabric, making it much softer.

Ethnic cloth, such as block-printed cottons or wax prints, definitely benefit from being prewashed. Many of these fabrics are dyed with natural materials, so the colour will run if the quilt gets damp. Wash different-coloured fabrics separately and rinse until the water runs clear. You should handwash any fabrics that are delicate or vintage before you use them, as dirt can be unkind to fabric and contribute to its wear and tear.

Finally, make sure you press any prewashed fabrics while they are still damp.

QUANTITIES
I have usually given approximate fabric requirements for each quilt, rather than exact quantities. This is partly because of the style of quilts I enjoy creating, but also because I believe it makes you more creative and intuitive if you aren't given a prescribed quantity for each fabric. As it is your quilt, surely you should be the one to choose which fabrics to use and where to place them? You can work out what you need by assessing what you already have – just like quilters did in the past – and adding to it if necessary.

Generally, the more seams you have in your quilt, the more fabric will be needed. Choose the size of the quilt you wish to make and then do a simple calculation. A finished quilt of 210 x 210cm would equal a total measurement of 4.41m. Round this up by a minimum of 25 per cent and the quantity needed is 5.5m. If the quilt has a larger number of seams, add at least 30 per cent, giving a total quantity of 5.7m. Any left-over fabric can be pieced for the backing or used for other projects.

WADDING

There are numerous types of wadding (or batting) from which to choose – from polyester to cotton and even soy. There are cotton and cotton blends, such as a cotton/bamboo mix, and wool. You can even choose organic wadding. Some types are lofty and light, while others are thin and weighty. Some are easier to hand-quilt, while some don't suit machine-quilting at all.

Wadding comes in different colours. For pale quilts, make sure you select bleached or natural-coloured wadding. For dark quilts, choose from the dark options available. This prevents fibres from showing through and contrasting with the quilt top – this is especially important if you are hand-quilting.

Wadding is sold by the metre or prepacked to fit standard bed sizes. If you are buying online, remember that European and American bed sizes are different, and if your mattress is particularly deep, you will need a larger piece of wadding. Measure your bed and go for a larger size if you are unsure. Check the manufacturer's instructions to see whether the wadding needs to be prewashed. You can wash the quilt after it is completed if you want to create an antique rumpled look and feel.

Your choice of wadding also depends on your method of quilting and the final look you want to achieve. Look on wadding manufacturers' websites to find out about each type before you choose. All quilters have their preference and quilting stores will sell what they think is right – which may not be right for you. After trying many different options, I have found that either organic cotton or a cotton/bamboo mix, depending on the quilt and who it is for, work best for my quilts.

Quilts were made long before wadding existed, so don't feel you have to use it if you have plenty of fabric that you want to use up. Many quilts were made using layers of cotton or other fabric that the makers had to hand to thicken the quilt. It is simply the layer that adds weight and warmth, so any fabric can be used, from an old blanket to cord or wool cloth. Just make sure the colour tone works with your quilt top and prewash if necessary.

THREAD

You will need two different types of thread to make a quilt. The first is a machine-sewing thread, which you will use for all sewing projects. This can be polyester, cotton-wrapped polyester or cotton. Any is fine, but try to buy a good-quality thread. For piecing, use a neutral colour that matches the tone of your quilt – either light or dark. The second is hand-sewing or quilting thread. It is less likely to twist or knot and, I think, gives a much nicer finish. Again, you can choose from polyester, polycotton or cotton.

I am a cotton lover and user. I generally use silk and cotton fabrics in my quilts, so I want to make sure my thread matches up to the look and feel of the textiles. I use Gütermann threads, but it is worth trying a couple of different brands to see which you like the feel of.

If you are hand-quilting, your choice of thread colour can add another level of personality to your quilt, so think about this at the planning stage. I use the same ivory thread to hand-quilt all of my quilts, irrespective of the colour of the quilt top. It unifies all the different fabrics and adds texture, but doesn't compete with the cloth or design. However, I have seen striking quilts that use vibrantly coloured thread to great effect. When you find the thread you like, buy lots of it: from my experience, it is always the colour they have run out of when you need more.

Toolkit

A sewer's toolkit is a marvellous thing; mine makes me feel creative, useful and prepared – plus, it is very nice to look at. It has travelled over the seas with me numerous times and, although I am well equipped, it doesn't contain an overwhelming number of tools. I have invested in high-quality equipment, so I have barely had to replace any – although the vacuum cleaner has suffered severe pin overload. Many of the tools

you need to make a quilt are necessary for other sewing pursuits, so you may already own them. Some have been created and designed solely for the purpose of quilt-making. Although I am not usually a fan of gadgets, these speciality tools ensure that cutting a quilt is fast and efficient, which gives you more time to create. Don't go crazy on gadgets, though – remember that the spirit of quilting is simply cutting up fabric and sewing it back together again, which doesn't need many tools at all. If you do need to purchase new tools, look for great quality and buy from specialists if you can. High-quality scissors can always be sharpened and repaired, and good pins will make your life a great deal easier.

The first three pieces of equipment below are specifically for making quilts. The others you would use for many other sewing projects. You can buy specialist equipment online or in your local haberdashery store. Look at the Resources on page 190 for some good suppliers.

CUTTING MAT

The smallest useful size for making quilts is A3. I use A0, but anywhere in between these sizes would be great – it depends on the space you have available. They come in either imperial and/or metric measurements, so make sure you buy the right kind for you.

ROTARY CUTTER

This makes cutting fabric so much easier. A rotary cutter is, in fact, a circular razor blade – so be careful. The most useful size is 45mm, but I also use 28mm for smaller pieces. I prefer Olfa as a brand, but make sure you find a cutter that feels comfortable in your hand, as they are all slightly different. When you buy your cutter, don't forget to buy some replacement blades.

For the left-handers among us (I am in this small but courageous group), choose a cutter that has a sliding mechanism over the blade instead of a grip.

QUILTER'S RULER

Made from transparent acrylic, a quilter's ruler makes accurate cutting easy. Rulers also come in a variety of sizes and are either metric or imperial, so make sure you buy one in the same system as your mat. You will need one at least 30cm long, although longer is better.

SEWING MACHINE

Your sewing machine doesn't need to be expensive and it doesn't need bells and whistles – trust me, it really doesn't. Do your research and some forward planning to choose the right one for you. They vary in price from £49 to £2,000 and beyond. Most sewers use only straight or zigzag stitch, so a basic sturdy machine from a well-known brand should suit.

I think it is important to choose a respected brand, firstly because the machine will come with a useful warranty, and secondly because it will be easier to find replacement parts and accessories. Visit your local sewing centre or a department store to find a machine that is comfortable to use, and make sure you have a lesson on using it before you take it home.

You can also buy excellent second-hand machines. If you do this, get it serviced before you start sewing to make sure it is at peak performance. Your local sewing centre should be able to do this for you, or you can search on the Internet for 'sewing machine service' and a number of mobile service companies should pop up.

If you are intending to machine-quilt, you will need a walking foot. You will also need a variety of needles, depending on the type of fabric you are planning to use – silk cloth requires finer needles than cotton.

OTHER SEWING EQUIPMENT

- IRON Choose one with a steam option for perfectly pressed seams.
- PINS I find long, fine pins the best. Make sure they have glass or metal heads, as plastic heads will melt if they come into contact with the iron.
- SCISSORS You will need sharp fabric scissors that you never use for paper. You will also need craft scissors for said paper, as well as a pair of embroidery or small scissors to snip threads. If you are left-handed, buy left-handed scissors.

'My sewing toolkit makes me feel creative, useful and prepared – plus it is very nice to look at.'

● SEAM RIPPER Essential for unpicking. Make sure it has a sharp blade and a comfortable handle.

● TAILOR'S CHALK OR ERASABLE PENCILS Buy a light and dark version of both, for numbering pieces, marking quilting patterns and tracing templates.

● NEEDLES You will need a variety of needles for quilting or hand-stitching: 'sharps' for general sewing, 'quilter's/betweens' for hand-quilting, and a small tapestry or darning needle for hand-tacking.

● THIMBLES There are several types – metal or leather. I use a leather one as it is more flexible and comfortable. I have also been known to use fabric plasters when the thimble has gone walkabout – they work a treat, too.

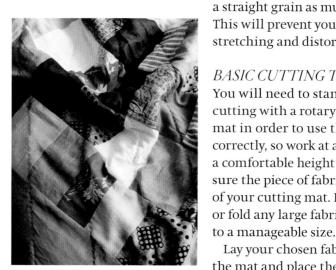

● FUSIBLE INTERFACING Iron this onto the back of knitted, fine or delicate fabrics to stabilize them.

● MASKING TAPE Use for marking quilting lines and for keeping fabric taut when tacking.

● MECHANICAL PENCIL, GRAPH PAPER AND SCALE RULER For drawing and adjusting your own designs.

● TAILOR'S TAPE MEASURE For measuring large pieces and slinging around your neck in order to appear professional.

● LONG METAL RULER For squaring up quilts and marking long, straight lines.

● CARDBOARD AND TRACING PAPER For templates.

● THICK RUBBER GLOVES, PLASTIC BUCKETS AND RUBBER BANDS For dyeing fabric.

Cutting

Before you cut any fabric, make sure that it is well pressed with the selvedges removed. You will cut most quilt designs using your rotary cutter, mat and ruler. Small or intricate pieces can be cut with fabric scissors, and curved pieces need to be cut with either fabric scissors or a rotary cutter with a small blade. None of this is difficult, but I know that cutting your fabric can be the most difficult part of starting your quilt. If you make a mistake, all is not lost –

you can always add a bit more, trim away the excess or use your 'mistake' as a creative inspiration.

Fabric has three grains: lengthways (warp); crossways (weft); and diagonal (bias). Both lengthways and crossways grains are 'straight' grains, which means they have very little stretch. Bias grain is cut at an angle, so it will give and stretch when sewn. Take care to cut your fabric on a straight grain as much as possible. This will prevent your quilt from stretching and distorting.

BASIC CUTTING TECHNIQUES
You will need to stand when cutting with a rotary cutter and mat in order to use the tools correctly, so work at a table that is a comfortable height for you. Make sure the piece of fabric fits the size of your cutting mat. If need be, cut or fold any large fabric pieces down to a manageable size.

Lay your chosen fabric flat on the mat and place the ruler on top of it. Use the lines on your cutting mat to make sure your fabric is straight. To cut the fabric, hold the blade of the rotary cutter flush against the ruler and always roll it away from you – for precision and, more importantly, safety. Always turn the cutting mat rather than yourself, and don't be tempted to cut across the fabric.

If you are left-handed, use the left-hand side of the cutting mat as your reference point and hold your ruler with your right hand. If you are right-handed, simply reverse this and use the right-hand side of the mat as your start point and hold your ruler with your left hand.

Keep your blades sharp and your cutting mat clean. As soon as your cutter starts to drag or not cut fabric cleanly, it is time to change the blade. Don't forget: absolutely always put the protective cover back on the cutter every time you put it down – get into the habit to avoid painful reminders.

CUTTING PIECED STRIPS
Press the pieced strip (see page 180) and place it right side up horizontally on the cutting mat. Straighten up the edges and cut the pieced strip to the required width. To cut a pieced strip on the

bias, first trim one edge at a 45° angle. Then cut strips at your chosen width at the same angle, using the edge of the ruler to keep your cutting line straight. You will use these techniques to create the Seminole quilt (see page 82).

CUTTING BIAS STRIPS

Trim one edge of a piece of fabric to create a true straight grain. Measure a 45° angle at a top corner and cut a bias edge as a guideline. Use your ruler to cut strips at your chosen width.

CUTTING TRIANGLES

Create half-square triangles by cutting across the diagonal of a square – be careful not to drag or distort the fabric when cutting across the grain. To cut triangles into quarters, cut diagonally across the first triangle.

CUTTING CURVES

Gradual curves can be cut with a 28mm rotary blade, but it is usually advisable to use fabric scissors. Always cut around the curve, not into it.

FUSSY CUTTING

If you have a piece of fabric that has a particular pattern as a central motif, you can cut your fabric to make the most of that. When cutting, use your quilting ruler to centre it – so you can see the motif as well as measure the correct cutting lines. You can use tailor's chalk or a dressmaker's pencil to help you work this out perfectly.

CUTTING WITH TEMPLATES

Line up your pattern or template along the straight grain of your fabric and trace around the edge with tailor's chalk or a dressmaker's pencil. Remember to flip templates that need opposites, or if the template needs to be asymmetrical, take care to trace them all on the right side of the fabric. Be precise in your tracing and cutting, and transfer any notches. It is just the same as cutting out a dress pattern.

If you are *wabi-sabi* by nature and don't mind imperfection, don't be put off making a quilt if your cutting isn't precise. If your corners don't

meet perfectly, but you love the outcome, then be happy with this. The Japanese have a philosophy of *kaizen*, which means continuous improvement, while being happy with what you have created now – and I love this idea. Just remember, it is the making that is important, not the perfect triangle.

Sewing techniques

Most quilters piece their quilt together using a sewing machine for ease and speed, although all of the quilts in the book can be hand-stitched if you prefer. The Postage Stamp quilt (see page 12) is an excellent quilt for teaching children to use a needle and thread, or make it your 'commuting' project. These are a few helpful quilt-sewing tips, which should make it simpler and less frustrating, and you less reliant on your seam ripper.

RIGHT SIDES FACING

Quite simple – always, always sew your fabrics together with their right sides facing. That is all you have to remember. We all make this mistake at least once when making a quilt, so have the seam ripper handy.

PIECING

This is the term used to describe sewing together all the different pieces in your quilt top. If you are making a quilt where all the pieces are a similar size – such as the String quilt (see page 106) – then cut all your pieces before you begin sewing. If they aren't, then you may want to cut a section and piece it together as you go – work at your own pace and confidence level.

SEAM ALLOWANCE

For teaching, I have always worked with a 1cm seam allowance. This is larger than standard, but I have found it makes piecing and freestyling far simpler for novices and people who make fewer than four quilts a year – most people. The vast majority of sewing machines have 1cm seam markers and it is a standard measurement for dressmaking patterns, which makes it easy to understand. I am not keen on new rules just because it is a different project – I am never really keen on rules if they make life complicated. The classic measurement derived from American quilts is ¼in or 6mm. You can, of course, adjust your quilt patterns if this is important to you. It is crucial to keep seam allowances consistent to make your blocks fit together. However, if you are one of the *wabi-sabi* people, then imperfect can indeed be perfect. If your quilt block is too small or too large, you can always add another piece of fabric, or trim off the excess. Don't let the seam allowance prevent you from starting or defeat you at the end!

PIECED STRIPS

Creating pieced strips can save time, as well as producing simple blocks that can be re-formed into new blocks. Sew your first two pieces of fabric together and press the seam towards the darker fabric. When you are piecing several strips together, reverse the direction each time you add a strip. This will keep your seams straight. Seams should always be pressed in the same direction if possible. The pieced strips can then be cut and re-pieced into a new pattern.

CHAIN PIECING

If you are sewing lots of small pieces together, it is far simpler to chain piece. Feed pairs of pieces through the sewing machine without lifting the presser foot or breaking the thread, so that it forms a chain. Once you have finished, cut the chain apart using your thread scissors.

TRIANGLE DOG EARS

When you have pieced triangles together, there will always be little 'dog ears' extending past the seams. Trim these away to reduce bulk and improve seam alignment.

SEWING CURVES

Sewing curves looks tricky, but if you have ever sewn a sleeve into a dress or shirt, you will know that it isn't. You will have a concave piece and a convex piece. With the convex piece on top, align the two edges together, match and pin the centre marks first, then pin the corners. Pin every 1cm, taking care to match the seamlines and gently ease in any fullness of the concave piece. Stitch along the curve without stretching or pulling it, and remove the pins as you sew. Press the seam towards the larger piece – it should lie flat without being clipped. Done.

PRESSING

Pressing is vital to a good-looking quilt. You need to have your iron on steam option, with the heat setting to suit your fabric choice. Lift your iron up and down to press, rather than sliding it across the quilt, as this can distort your blocks.

I generally press the seams before I have to turn the block and sew on top of a seam I have already sewn. You could make a pressing board to sit next to your sewing machine using MDF, wadding and cotton fabric, or buy a portable mini ironing board. This means you won't have to get up and down constantly – but do what suits you best.

Press your seamlines open first and then choose the direction in which you want them to lie. Pick one direction and try to stick with it. I choose a different solution depending on the quilt. Many seams mean more planning and care. You don't want too many seams overlapping, as this can make part of the quilt bulky and difficult to stitch through. You also don't want to have darker fabrics showing through lighter fabrics. Sometimes you can choose one method and easily stick with it. At other times you will have to compromise – it obviously isn't life-threatening, but a little planning and care should avoid too many glitches.

For small seams, try finger-pressing them using your thumbnail, a hera marker or a mini wooden iron (available at haberdasheries). You will need to press the seams with an iron at a later point, but finger-pressing works really well on short seams.

'Chain piecing is a simple, time-saving technique when you need to join lots of small pieces together.'

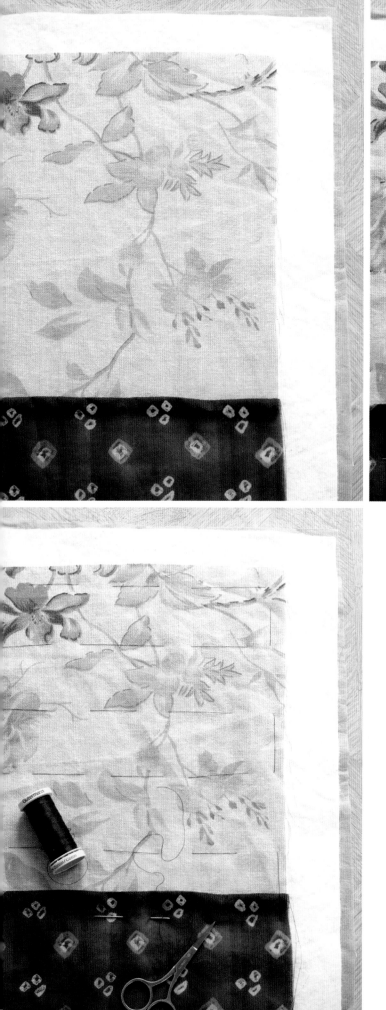

Building your quilt

You have planned, designed, cut and pieced your quilt top. You have chosen your wadding and sewn together your quilt backing – you are almost there. You just need to assemble the three layers together so that you can quilt and bind your masterpiece.

Your wadding and backing need to be at least 10cm larger all round than your quilt top. As you pin, or tack, your quilt together, the quilt top can move a little bit. The excess backing and wadding allow for this movement without compromising your quilt top.

If your wadding has been folded, open it out flat and leave it for a few hours to relax the wrinkles before you assemble the layers.

Press your backing and lay it, right side down, on a clean, hard surface – either the floor or table. If you have made your quilt backing out of a mixture of fabric, decide if there is a natural top and bottom to it – the direction it will be on the bed – and allow for this when assembling the layers. Carefully smooth the backing flat and use masking tape to secure it to the surface to keep it taut. Place the tape at points along the sides of the backing but not on the corners.

Lay your piece of wadding on top of your quilt backing, smoothing it out and matching the edges. If the wadding is larger than the backing, trim it down to match.

Press your quilt top until it is perfect, doing a final check for any loose threads as you do so. Lay the quilt top right side up on the wadding, centred on the backing. Use a ruler to ensure that the quilt top is squared up.

PINNING OR TACKING

Traditionally, the layers of a quilt are temporarily pinned or tacked together to prepare it (and you) for permanent quilting or tying together. It is important to keep the three layers taut as you quilt, to avoid puckering or creasing. There are three methods you can use, so try a couple of them to find the one that works for you.

You can use long, fine quilting pins – they are inexpensive and abundant, and allow you to use any method of quilting. Obviously, they can (and will) fall out when you move the quilt and you may prick yourself as you work, but you can pin a quilt together relatively quickly and simply.

Alternatively, you can hand-tack the quilt using a long darning needle or a curved needle. You need to create a grid and tack rows of long stitches, horizontally and vertically, approximately 10cm apart. Long-arm quilters can also provide this service. It is difficult to machine-quilt a quilt that has been tacked, but a tacked quilt is easier to pick up and put down. I usually hand-tack my quilts now, after many years of pinning them, as I find it simpler and more secure.

Finally, you can use quilter's safety pins. They are curved in shape so are much easier to use than a standard safety pin, but they are more expensive

than quilting pins. You pin the quilt together using the same method as for quilting pins, but you will need to preplan your quilting lines if you are intending to machine-quilt.

Working from the centre out, tack, pin or safety-pin the three layers together. Keep smoothing the fabric as you work. Tacking stitches should be approximately 5cm long, whereas pins and safety pins should be inserted at around 10cm intervals.

Remember to remove your pins or tacking stitches after you have finished quilting.

Quilting

As with all aspects of making a quilt, there are many choices of quilting method. Each requires different skills and patience, and they will all give your quilt a different look and feel. The functional aspect of quilting is to hold the three layers together to create a robust, usable object – but, of course, it is so much more than that. Your stitching can be decorative or functional – preplanned or free-form. Each quilt design will offer a different opportunity for creativity. A quilt that is heavily hand-quilted will have a completely different feel from one that is long-arm quilted or sparsely machine-quilted. There is also the triangle of time, inclination and available funds to consider. Everyone will have a different mix of each – and what will be inspiring for some will be absolute water torture for others.

MARKING QUILT LINES

Before you start to quilt, you need to plan (or not) your quilting lines. For straight lines, you can use masking tape. I apply this after I have tacked the quilt together. For circles or curves, you can use tailor's chalk for darker cloths or other erasable pencils (test these on your fabric before you use them). You can also use stencils and a fabric pouncer – a chalk powder – to create patterns.

I find this works best if you concentrate on a small area at a time, as the chalk can brush or wear off.

You can, of course, quilt without any pattern – use your eyes, stitch close to seams, or quilt in the ditch to give an overall design.

HAND-QUILTING

This is the original method of quilting and I love it. Your quilt will be soft and vintage in look and feel, as your stitching lines will be broken, and your eyes and hands will have created the effect rather than a man-made machine.

Hand-quilting is easy (if you can sew on a button, you can most certainly hand-quilt), but it can be time-consuming. Don't be put off by the quality of antique or 'professional' quilts. Your stitching doesn't need to be impossibly tiny or perfect – you just need to have a go. You will soon find a natural rhythm and size of stitch that you are comfortable with and enjoy. If you are new to hand-quilting, start with a larger quilting needle and always use hand-quilting thread. This will help to prevent knots from forming, feel better to use and create a much lovelier finish.

I use a simple running stitch in the design of my choice. I either preplan my stitching lines using masking tape or tailor's pencils, or I just sketch one curved line and free-form quilt following that. I don't necessarily plan how much I am going to quilt, either – it is whatever I feel suits the quilt and how much time I want to spend on it.

Many quilters like to use hoops or frames to keep their quilt taut. I generally just quilt in my lap, starting from one side and working across, keeping it smooth as I go. Quilting this way sometimes distorts the quilt slightly, but I am happy with that – the quilts from Gee's Bend are positively wonky but, I think, all the more beautiful because of it. Just find a way that suits you.

LONG-ARM QUILTING

You can have your quilt long-arm quilted instead of hand- or machine-quilting the quilt yourself. This gives a flatter and more refined finish than hand-quilting and more precise designs than domestic machine-quilting. Instead of assembling your quilt layers yourself, simply send the parts of your quilt to the long-arm quilters, or make an appointment to visit – it is worth doing this to see the choice of designs and services available.

Long-arm quilters can tack the quilt for you to hand- or machine-quilt yourself, or they will fully quilt it with a design of your choice. They can also attach and hand-finish the binding, if that is one job too many. They offer a huge variety of quilting designs and thread colours, which add to the feel of your quilt. They can even provide wadding – just make sure it is the type you want to use.

To find a long-arm quilter, type the term into a search engine and look through the websites to see what options are offered and the creative styles, as they vary hugely. I have tried a substantial number of long-arm quilters but now use one that I return to again and again, because they understand my style of quilt-making, as well as provide fantastic workmanship (they are listed in the Resources on page 190).

'Each quilting method requires different skills and patience, and will result in a different look and feel.'

MACHINE-QUILTING

The most difficult part of machine-quilting is the potential for 'wrestling' your quilt through the sewing machine. However, if you are a 'competent' sewer, you can machine-quilt a queen-sized quilt easily on a standard sewing machine. For larger quilts, roll up one side of the quilt so that it fits into the circular gap of your machine. Quilt as much as you can on one side and then turn it around, roll up the other side and continue. Make sure you have space around your machine and clean surfaces.

Machine-quilting is faster than hand-quilting and is a low-cost alternative to long-arm quilting. It is cleaner and crisper in feel, and definitely has a place for certain projects. If you are more than 'competent' with your sewing machine, you can delve into the world of free-motion quilting, too, which gives a close alternative finish to long-arm quilting. Remember to plan your thread colours and use quilting cotton if you can. You will need to use a walking foot for machine-quilting and a darning foot for free-motion quilting.

The art of binding

There are more ways to bind a quilt than you can imagine, and everyone is passionate about their own preferred method. I like fine binding, but some people like chunky binding. I love sharp and square corners; some of you prefer rounded corners. I particularly love neatly spaced slip stitching; this will be excruciating for others.

Binding encloses the quilt edges. So, on a practical level, it is what keeps the quilt durable. From a design perspective, it provides your last opportunity to add something special to your quilt to tie the fabric and design together.

You can use many fabrics to bind your quilt – from off-cuts from the quilt top to men's ties, which could be purpose-made for the task, or you can buy something new. You can also buy ready-made binding in everything from satin to Liberty-print cotton and velvet. Wait until you have finished your quilt top and backing before you decide on the binding. Personally, I don't want the binding to be a statement in my quilt designs; I prefer it to slip away into the background – but it is up to you.

MAKING BINDING

Binding can either be cut across the straight grain or on the bias. Cutting on the straight grain will require less fabric and so will be more economical; the binding will also be a little easier to cut and piece together. However, cutting on the bias allows some stretch for the corners, which is helpful if you want to make round corners. After making many quilts, I don't see a great benefit in cutting binding on the bias, but it is your choice.

Trim the edges of your quilt so that they are all straight and square (see step 1, opposite) – don't be tempted to overtrim if there is a slight wobble in your lines. Measure all four sides and add an extra 15–20cm to determine the length of binding required. Cut your binding fabric, straight or on the bias, into strips 5cm wide, incorporating a 1cm seam allowance on each edge. You can cut wider or narrower binding if you prefer.

Join all the strips together, end to end, to form a continuous length. Fold the strip in half along its length, with wrong sides together, and press.

ATTACHING THE BINDING

Leave about 5–10cm of the binding strip free. Start in the centre of one side of the quilt and, with right sides together, pin one raw edge of the binding to the edge of the quilt top, through all layers. The folded edge of the binding strip will be facing towards the inside of the quilt (see step 2).

DEALING WITH CORNERS

For crisp, square corners, pin all the way around the quilt and, when you get to a corner, fold the binding strip to one side and then back on top of itself to make a triangle. This gives you a mitred corner (see steps 3–4).

Machine-sew around the quilt with a 1cm seam allowance. Stop about 0.5cm from the edge of the corner and then start the next seam 0.5cm after the corner (see step 5).

For softer-looking round corners, pin all the way around the quilt, carefully easing the binding around the corners, until you reach the start.

Machine-sew around the quilt with a 1cm seam allowance. Stop about 0.5cm from the edge of the corner, backstitch, and then slowly stitch around the corner, easing the binding as you go.

Whichever style of corner you have chosen, when you get near the beginning, backstitch, and remove the quilt from the sewing machine. Trim off the excess binding, leaving a 1cm turn-in, and fold and pin the binding under itself. Hand-sew the last few stitches (see step 6).

FINISHING THE BINDING

Fold the binding over to the reverse of the quilt and pin it in place, turning the raw edge under by 1cm as you do so. Finally, hand-stitch the binding to the quilt backing using invisible slip stitch – or another hand-stitch if you prefer (see steps 7–8).

NOTE

It is possible (though trickier) to machine-sew the binding to the front and back in one go. You will require lots of pins and a careful eye to ensure that you catch all the layers. Another option is to send it to the long-arm quilters and let them do it for you.

'I generally prefer
narrow binding
that doesn't
steal any of the
limelight from the
quilt top itself.'

Quilt care

I hope that your quilts will be used on beds, sofas and people. Of course, at some stage, they will need cleaning, but this can be done easily if you are careful and methodical. To reduce overcleaning, start by shaking your quilts when you are changing the bed. Vacuum quilts regularly to prevent dirt from settling into the fabric. Spot-clean any marks or spills with a gentle detergent and minimal water.

I always handwash quilts by soaking them in the bath. I don't trust washing machines, although I know that you can wash cotton quilts on a delicate setting. When handwashing a quilt, ensure that the water is lukewarm and leave your quilt to soak. Add gentle quilt soap if you want to, but bear in mind that it will have to be rinsed out completely. If the water is a little murky, drain it and refill the tub with fresh water. Repeat this if necessary until the water is clear. Drain the bath and leave the quilt to release all the excess water. Fabric is fragile when wet, so lift the quilt out using a sheet. Always dry quilts flat, as hanging them can stretch and tear the fibres. I often wash my quilts on a hot summer's day and then lay them outside in the shade to dry. Once the top of the quilt feels dry, turn it over for the backing to dry thoroughly. If your quilt is silk or wool, you can have it dry-cleaned – just make sure you choose a top-notch dry-cleaner.

GLOSSARY

APPLIQUÉ: The technique of attaching a piece of fabric onto a larger piece of contrasting fabric. To prevent fraying, the edges of the appliqué may be turned under and sewn with a straight stitch, or just sewn down with a blanket or satin stitch.

BACKING: A piece of cloth forming the underside of a quilt. This may be several pieces sewn together.

BEARDING: When wadding fibres migrate up through the quilt top. Using dark wadding in a dark quilt and vice versa reduces the visibility of the fibres.

BIAS: The diagonal grain of a fabric – at 45° to the warp and weft grains.

BINDING: The strip of folded fabric used to cover the raw edges of a quilt. It can be cut on the straight or bias grain.

BLOCK: An individual design unit within a quilt, usually in the form of a square of pieced patchwork that is put together with other blocks to make a quilt. A block may be any size, from very small to big enough to cover a bed.

CHAIN PIECING: Sewing together pairs of units in a continuous sequence, without lifting the sewing machine presser foot or breaking the thread.

DARNING FOOT: A sewing-machine foot, usually round or oval and clear plastic, used with the feed dogs lowered for free-motion quilting.

FREE-MOTION QUILTING: Machine-quilting with a darning foot and the feed dogs lowered. The stitching can be in any direction and may be simple wavy lines or very complex patterns.

FUSIBLE INTERFACING: Fabric that is impregnated with heat-activated adhesive. It is used for stabilizing knitted or fine, delicate fabrics.

FUSSY CUTTING: Cutting around a specific motif or design to use as a feature within a block or quilt.

GRAIN: The direction in which warp and weft threads lie in a woven fabric; warp threads run parallel to the selvedge and perpendicular to the weft threads.

HAND-QUILTING: Sewing the quilting stitches in a quilt by hand rather than with a sewing machine.

HEMMING: The process by which a raw edge is turned under and sewn down with small stitches. Hemming is used to attach binding to the back of a quilt.

LOFT: The thickness or puffiness of quilt wadding, which varies from very thin to very puffy.

MACHINE-QUILTING: Sewing the quilting stitches with a sewing machine rather than by hand. Even though the sewing machine became widely used in the mid-1800s, hand-quilting remained prevalent until the late 1900s.

PAPER PIECING: A technique whereby pieces of fabric are tacked and sewn to a paper foundation to form a quilt block.

PATCHWORK: Sewing together smaller pieces of fabric to create a larger piece.

PIECING: The making of the quilt top by sewing smaller pieces of fabric together.

QUILT: The 'sandwich' consisting of three layers: the quilt top is decorative; the backing is usually, but not always, plain; the wadding provides warmth and loft.

QUILT-MAKING: The entire process of making a quilt – piecing and quilting.

QUILTING: Either the act of sewing together of the layers of a quilt (the top, wadding and backing), or the term used for the stitching that holds the layers together. It is both practical, in order to stabilize the quilt, and decorative.

QUILTING BEE: A social event involving friends and neighbours gathered to complete several quilts in a single day instead of weeks or months.

RIGHT SIDE: The top layer, or the side that will be seen when stitched into place.

RUNNING STITCH: A simple stitch used for tacking, quilting and piecing. The needle goes in and out of the cloth, usually making two or more stitches at a time.

SEAM: The join formed when two pieces of fabric are sewn together.

SEAM ALLOWANCE: The amount of fabric allowed within a pattern where seams join.

SELVEDGE: The woven edge along each side of the fabric to prevent it from fraying.

SEWING MACHINE: Patented in 1846, a sewing machine allows quilters to piece fabric quickly.

SLIP STITCH: A hidden stitch that creates an almost invisible seam, used for binding or closing edges.

SQUARING UP: Carefully trimming blocks to make them perfectly square.

STASH: A quilter's fabric collection.

STITCH IN THE DITCH: Nearly invisible stitches that follow the seams of the pieced top, within the seam itself.

STRAIGHT STITCH: The plain machine stitch used to join seams.

TACKING: Sewing large removable stitches by hand or machine in order to hold the quilt layers together.

TEMPLATE: A precisely measured, reusable model, often of cardboard or plastic, to size individual pieces of fabric.

TOP: The uppermost layer of a quilt, which is usually the decorative side.

WADDING: Also known as batting, this is the inner layer between the quilt top and the backing that adds insulation, loft and warmth. Originally cotton, wool or polyester, newer types of wadding are made from silk, cotton/polyester blends, soy fibres and bamboo.

WALKING FOOT: A sewing-machine foot that feeds fabric from the top while the feed dogs feed it from the bottom, preventing shifting and puckering.

WARP: The threads that run across the length of woven fabric.

WEAVE: The way a fabric is constructed. There are three basic weave patterns: plain, twill and satin.

WEFT: The filling threads that cross the warp and run across the width of woven fabric.

RESOURCES

MUSEUMS AND GALLERIES

The museums and galleries listed either specialize in quilts or have significant galleries dedicated to the craft of cloth. Look at their websites as well – many have online resources.

UK

AMERICAN MUSEUM IN BRITAIN
Claverton Manor
Bath BA2 7BD
americanmuseum.org
The only museum of American decorative and folk art outside the USA.

BRITISH MUSEUM
Great Russell Street
London WC1B 3DG
britishmuseum.org

THE CLOTHWORKERS' CENTRE FOR THE STUDY AND CONSERVATION OF TEXTILES AND FASHION
Blythe House
23 Blythe Road
London W14 0QX
This is the new textile learning centre of the Victoria & Albert Museum.

QUILT MUSEUM AND GALLERY
St Anthony's Hall
Peasholme Green
York YO1 7PW
quiltmuseum.org.uk
Britain's first museum dedicated to the history of British quilt-making and textile arts.

VICTORIA & ALBERT MUSEUM
Cromwell Road
London SW7 2RL
vam.ac.uk

USA

AMERICAN FOLK ART MUSEUM
2 Lincoln Square
New York, NY 10023
folkartmuseum.org

TEXTILE MUSEUM
2320 S Street, NW
Washington DC
20008-4008
textilemuseum.org

CANADA

TEXTILE MUSEUM OF CANADA
55 Centre Avenue
Toronto
textilemuseum.ca

FRANCE

MUSÉE DES TISSUS ET DES ARTS DECORATIFS
30–34 rue de la Charité
69002 Lyon
musee-des-tissus.com

INDIA

THE CALICO MUSEUM OF TEXTILES
Sarabhai House
Shahi Baug, 380004
Ahmedabad
thebharat.com/tourism/museum/amhadabad.html

NEW ZEALAND

TE PAPA
Cable Street
Wellington
tepapa.govt.nz

LONG-ARM QUILTERS

UK

THE QUILT ROOM
37–39 High Street
Dorking
Surrey RH4 1AR
quiltroom.co.uk
This is the company I use.

ONLINE STORES

africanfabric.co.uk
The best source for African fabrics.

anansevillage.com
Fair-trade African fabrics.

beckfordsilk.co.uk
For a good range of un-dyed silk and silk velvet.

clothaholics.com
Japanese indigo cottons and vintage kimonos.

etsy.com
folksy.com
Both sites are excellent resources for antique and vintage cloth, as well as new cloth from around the world – look out for block-printed cottons.

habutextiles.com
Fantastic selection of Japanese wool, silk and cotton.

ichiroya.com
Antique and vintage Japanese cloth and kimonos.

kimonoboy.com
Japanese folk textiles.

lesindiennes.com
Beautiful hand-block-printed cottons that you can order in 5m bolts.

lin-net.com
Another lovely Japanese textile offering.

merchantandmills.com
All the haberdashery and high-quality tools you could want.

parna.co.uk
For excellent vintage
hemp and linen.

uzbek-craft.com
Ikat and Suzani fabric.

STORES
UK
CLOTH HOUSE
47 Berwick Street
London W1F 8SJ and
98 Berwick Street
London W1F 0QJ
clothhouse.com
Fabrics from around the
world, and everything
you could want – on the
proviso that it is beautiful
and made responsibly.
This store is perfect.

THE CLOTH SHOP
290 Portobello Road
London W10 5TE
theclothshop.net
An Aladdin's cave of
intriguing fabric and
cloth, including antique
Swedish rag rugs, Indian
silk shawls, cashmere
and wool blankets from
Scotland and antique
Welsh blankets.

JEN JONES
Pontbrendu Llanybydder
Ceredigion
SA40 9UJ
jen-jones.com
The largest collection and
stock of antique Welsh
quilts and Welsh blankets
anywhere in the world.

JOHN LEWIS
johnlewis.com
For an excellent range of
sewing machines. Good
for thread and needles,
too. Buy online or visit
your local branch.

LIBERTY OF LONDON
220 Regent Street
London W1B 5AH
liberty.co.uk
For Liberty fabric, and
also for Kaffe Fassett
cloth, and a small selection
of other Rowan fabrics.

MACCULLOCH & WALLIS
25–26 Dering Street
London W1S 1AT
macculloch-wallis.co.uk
This company has been
around for ever and has
everything you could
possibly want for quilting.

ORGANIC TEXTILE
COMPANY
43–45 Maengwyn Street
Machynlleth SY20 8EL
organiccotton.biz
Great selection of organic
cotton. Ordering a swatch
set is a great idea.

RIBA BOOKSHOPS
ribabookshops.com
I find architecture books
a great resource when
designing quilts. There
are three Royal Institute
of British Architects
bookshops in London.

RUSSELL AND CHAPPLE
68 Drury Lane
London WC2B 5SP
russellandchapple.co.uk
Produces excellent-quality
linen and cotton for a good
price. You can buy online,
but I think it is worth
visiting the store at least
once to gather samples.

SELVEDGE DRY GOODS
162 Archway Road
London N6 5BB
selvedge-drygoods.org
Lovely artisan textile
goods, as well as a good
selection of books.

TOBIAS AND THE ANGEL
68 White Hart Lane
London SW13 0PZ
tobiasandtheangel.com
Angel carries her own
hand-printed fabric and
an extensive collection of
antique and vintage finds.

V V ROULEAUX
102 Marylebone Lane
London W1U 2QD
vvrouleaux.com
For all your passementerie
needs. Also available at
John Lewis and Liberty.

USA
PURL SOHO
459 Broome Street
New York, NY 10013
purlsoho.com
A great fabric and yarn
shop that curates its range
very well. Almost all of it is
available online.

SRI THREADS
18 Eckford Street, #8
Brooklyn, NY 11222
srithreads.com
Expensive but worth it for
something very special
from Japan or India.
Open by appointment
only, although you can
buy some pieces online.

INSPIRATIONS
These are places that
inspired me for this book.
Some I have visited once,
others at least a dozen
times. They have been
the trigger for at least one
design or thought. Try to
visit as many exhibitions
and galleries as you can.
Enjoy gardens, beaches
and waterways at all times
of the year – in winter, they
are at their most two-
dimensional. Let them fill

you up and spark ideas
for colour, line or even a
completely new design.

BARBARA HEPWORTH
MUSEUM & SCULPTURE
GARDEN
Barnoon Hill
St Ives
Cornwall TR26 1AD
tate.org.uk/stives/
hepworth/
Hepworth sculptures in
bronze, stone and wood
displayed in the museum
and garden, along with
paintings, drawings and
archive material.

COLD PRESS GALLERY
18–20 Albert Street
Holt
Norfolk NR25 6HX
www.thecoldpress.com
Exhibitions of recent
publications made in their
Studio, as well as the work
of invited artists, furniture
and the applied arts.

DITCHLING MUSEUM
OF ART + CRAFT
Lodge Hill Lane
Ditchling
East Sussex BN6 8SP
ditchlingmuseumartcraft.
org.uk
Focuses on the artists and
craftspeople who made
Ditchling a creative hub
in the twentieth century.

GREAT DIXTER
Northiam
Rye
East Sussex TN31 6PH
greatdixter.co.uk
Historic house and garden.

THE HEPWORTH
WAKEFIELD
GALLERY WALK
Wakefield WF1 5AW
A completely different take
on Barbara Hepworth's
work but equally stunning
as the Museum & Sculpture
Garden above.

KELMSCOTT MANOR
Kelmscott, Lechlade
Gloucestershire GL7 3HJ
kelmscottmanor.org.uk
The summer home of
William Morris. Probably
his most personal house.

KETTLE'S YARD
Castle Street
Cambridge CB3 0AQ
kettlesyard.co.uk
Distinctive collection of
twentieth-century art, and
a gallery of contemporary
and modern art.

SISSINGHURST CASTLE
Biddenden Road, near
Cranbrook, Kent
TN17 2AB
nationaltrust.org.uk/
sissinghurst-castle
World-renowned gardens.

TATE BRITAIN
Millbank
London SW1P 4RG
tate.org.uk/visit/tate-
britain
Where my *A World of Quilts*
adventure began.

TURNER CONTEMPORARY
RENDEZVOUS
Margate, Kent
CT9 1HG UK
turnercontemporary.org
Contemporary and
historical art exhibitions.

ACKNOWLEDGEMENTS

It was such a joy to make this book.
Thank you, Cath, for your amazing
photographs again. Each quilt tells its
story beautifully because of your images
and who you are. Thank you, Zia, for
wonderful editing. You make my
overexcited words calm (and so much
better) and it is always so very easy.
The three of us had such fun shooting
together and everything looks and feels
better because of that. Thank you, Claire,
for your calm and supportive approach – it
has made the process so much easier and
gentler. Thank you, Jacqui and Jo, for the
opportunity to create a book for you again.
I am so thrilled with what it has become.

To my Ed – thank you for putting up
with me writing and making on weekends,
holidays and in the very small hours of
the mornings. It took over my life for six
months and you waited quietly for my
mind to return to everyday matters.

Last, but definitely not least, thank
you to the makers – the women and
men whose stories and lives gave me
the opportunity to research, relish and
interpret their creativity and celebrate
their choices.

CREDITS
The author and publisher would like to
thank Loaf (www.loaf.com) and The White
Company (www.thewhitecompany.com)
for the kind loan of their beds and bed
linen for our photography.

Additional photography
Debi Treloar: pages 29, 32–3, 67, 71, 127,
131 and 174.
Michael Wicks: pages 15, 19, 25, 31, 37, 43,
49, 55, 63, 69, 75, 79, 85, 91, 97, 103, 109, 115,
123, 129, 135, 141, 147, 153 and 161.